Up Country

WITH JAMES GLADSTONE

Up Country

WITH JAMES GLADSTONE

Illustrated by
KATHRYN LAMB
Introduction by
PHIL ARCHER

A Collection of Columns from
Big Farm Weekly 1977–1987

ANDRE DEUTSCH

First published in 1988 by
André Deutsch Limited
105–106 Great Russell Street
London WC1B 3LJ

ISBN 0 233 98342 2

Typeset by CentraCet, Cambridge
Printed in Great Britain by
Billing & Sons, Worcester

Contents

Introduction

I met an agricultural journalist once. He was wearing a rather snappy suit and I managed to get a good look at his hands. I reckon you can tell a lot from a man's hands, and this chap's told me that the nearest he got to a farm was buying his polythene wrapped spuds off the supermarket shelf.

I read his stuff that week in one of the farming mags and it was competent enough – the green pound, M3, mcas, not the kind of prose I look forward to reading of an evening when Jill and I are sitting in front of the fire at Brookfield.

No, for the evenings I save up the articles which are written by farmers, for farmers, from one bloke with mud on his boots and a cow outside about to calve, to another. There's a distinguished line of farmer/writers in this country from A. G. Street onwards, and it seems to me this man Gladstone is currently running with the ball.

I don't say I always agree with him (in fact the more I learn about his suckler herd the more I wonder if he hasn't got a screw loose), or that he always makes comfortable reading (guess what we'd had for supper the night I read 'Real Farmers Don't Eat Quiche') but farming's a solitary occupation and, apart from The Bull and the odd NFU meeting or agricultural show, there's not much chance to swap ideas.

Thanks then, James Gladstone, for showing me there's someone out there who makes as many mistakes as I do (get rid of the suckler herd, that's my advice, James) and who can actually laugh at them.

Here in Borsetshire we try to keep quiet about our mistakes like that uneven, no, bald patch in my wheat the other side of Lakey Hill. It only takes one farmer to see it (name of Grundy, usually) and you hardly dare show your face in The Bull for a month. And I have to tell Jill not to invite the Aldridges over for Sunday lunch or I'll have Brian crowing over me until dessert.

Eurocrats, politicians and all the others who make a living out of confusing us are his targets, and when Gladstone raises his voice against them I feel I'm shouting too. Jill reckons it's very good for the blood pressure. Oh, and have I mentioned he makes me laugh? That's no mean feat according to my family. What I'm trying to say is that, if I met Gladstone, I'd probably like the look of his hands.

Philip Archer
Brookfield Farm, Ambridge
Dorset
March 1988

How Green Is Your Wellie?

IN WHICH WE EXAMINE THE DIFFERENCE BETWEEN
THE SON OF THE SOIL ON THE ONE HAND, AND THE
AGRI-BUSINESSMAN ON THE OTHER

Are You a Real Farmer?

For my fortieth birthday I was given a book called *Real Men Don't Eat Quiche* – a fairly barbed present for someone like me who considers quiche to be a hearty lunch. This is an American book which sets out to remind the American male how to stay hairy-chested and masculine, qualities which the feminist movement has apparently been eroding over the years.

Its title and attitude is based on the premise that John Wayne 'could never have taken Normandy, Iwo Jima, Korea, the Gulf of Tonkin and the entire Wild West on a diet of quiche and salad!' And who could argue with that?

Tacked on to the end of the British edition are a couple of pages entitled 'True Brit, Real Man and The Land' which try, but fail, to describe the qualities that go to make up a Real Farmer.

Simplistically it claims that Real Farmers grub up hedges, spray everything in sight and shoot anything that survives the sprays. 'Dan Archer eats quiche,' it concludes. 'But Joe Grundy is Real.'

Those of us who actually farm know that the whole thing is much more subtle than that. How would you tell the difference between the Real Farmer and the Quiche Farmer? Here are a few ideas for starters.

Real Farmers don't use low-ground-pressure vehicles; they have enough horse-power around to haul themselves out of any swamp. And they don't use direct drills; they use the biggest, heaviest reversible plough they can lay their hands on.

Real Farmers don't have automatic cluster removal.

Real Farmers don't make big bales.

I'm not sure, but it could be that Real Farmers make hay, not silage.

Real Farmers certainly don't wear green Hunter boots, down-filled gilets, deer-stalkers or T-shirts in summer. They do wear overalls.

Real Farmers have collies, not labradors.

Real Farmers never call the vet.

Real Farmers do most of their drilling by headlights.

Real Farmers farm heavy clay, rock, or anywhere north of a line drawn from Scarborough to Barrow-in-Furness. Hampshire and Sussex are particularly Quiche agricultural areas.

Real Farmers don't read farming papers.

Do You Pass the Quiche Test?

How can you tell the difference between the Real and the Quiche in farming? Here's the definitive guide, based on farmers' own contributions.

In the office . . .

REAL FARMERS	QUICHE FARMERS
Never write letters.	Employ secretaries.
Don't know a hectare from a litre.	Pronounce the 'e' in 'tonnes'.
Budget on the back of the barn door with a rusty nail.	Programme the computer to estimate returns on capital employed.
Must always have a discount.	Say 'Book it, will you?'

Threaten three times a week to leave the NFU.	Try to make you join the BFS.
Look after the pennies.	Have cash-flow problems and stockbrokers.
File bumph behind the clock on the mantelpiece.	File bumph in files.

Clothes are a major clue, of course . . .

REAL FARMERS	QUICHE FARMERS
Wear vests and wool shirts, even in summer.	Take their shirts off to boost their suntans.
Tuck their shirts inside their underpants.	Buy bikini briefs in Harrods.
Have turn-ups on the trousers of the best tweed suit.	Wear shorts.
Always keep their heads covered.	Wear sunglasses.
Tie their shoes and boots with leather laces.	Wear skiing socks in their green wellies.

But the real give-aways are in the way they farm . . .

REAL FARMERS	QUICHE FARMERS
Have always sold their grain £2 better than you.	'Market' grain through a co-operative.
Can't stand Q cabs.	Listen to Wimbledon on the tractor radio.
Bale all their straw.	Burn everything.
Put the best beast and three-lamb ewes by the road: keep the pot-bellied Friesian heifer and toothless old sheep out of sight.	Have all animals under cover, on slats, invisible.
Can't operate without stick, cap and baler twine.	Have a brown hat for racing.
Put up barbed wire.	Complain about trespassers.
Put up barbed wire.	Hang gates.
Put up barbed wire.	Erect the Council's footpath signs.
Change a tractor when the last one's knackered.	Change tractors according to a complex formula relating allowances to depreciation.
Have overdrafts.	Have overdrafts.
Have names for all their cows.	Have names for all their herds.
Don't trust AI.	Don't trust bulls.

Wives contributed most of this section, called 'food, drink and recreation' . . .

REAL FARMERS

Drink cider, beer, whisky.

Have dinner at midday.
Suspect food cooked with wine, garlic, pepper or rice.
Have never heard of muesli.
Use ferrets.

Kill rats with terriers.

Take days off for market and funerals.
Played club rugby when young.
Never keep domestic pets, and certainly not ponies.

QUICHE FARMERS

Drink vodka, gin, dry white wine.
Dine at night.
Cook food with wine, garlic, etc.
Prefer fruit juice for breakfast.
Belong to a shooting syndicate.
Have contracts with rodent control operatives.
Insist on two holidays a year.

Never played anything outside a casino.
Have horses in training at Lambourn.

And lastly the really personal bit . . .

REAL FARMERS

Go to the barber on market day.
Shave after 'bait' (breakfast).

Have blackheads.
Would not be seen dead washing car, boots, collie, hair.
Hate foreigners.

Never go to a doctor.
Shoot foxes.
Call the wife 'missus' or 'mum'.
Expect wives to be Mrs Beeton in the kitchen, the Princess of Wales when out and Jackie Collins in bed.

QUICHE FARMERS

Make appointments with hairdressers.
Shave a second time when dining out.
Use deodorant.
Power wash tractors.

Are most impressed by Schleswig-Holstein.
Complain about BUPA fees.
Shoot driven partridges.
Call the wife 'darling'.

Expect the first wife to be Jackie Collins in bed, the second to look like the Princess and the third to cook like Mrs Beeton.

Delia Smith
Nigella Lawson
JORDAN

The Real Farmer's Nightmare

The wife of a local Real Farmer came back from lifting the last of the potatoes the other afternoon to find her husband at one end of the lawn with the three-furrow reversible poised to bite.

You do not live within a mile of Greenham Common without learning how to handle threats like that; without a moment's hesitation she prostrated herself in front of the tractor.

The negotiations which ensued made SALT look like a meeting of the local whist drive committee. Eventually, Real Farmer agreed to spare the lawn in exchange for five acres of the pony paddock. He turned his tractor and plough around and she went off to unload ten tons of fertilizer with honours intact bilaterally.

He won much beery sympathy at the bar of the Happy Heifer in the evening, however. He seems to be suffering from a virus which has never been more widespread than this year due to the good weather. He's been ploughing and discing, harrowing and drilling ever since he got off the combine and he cannot stop; he thinks of nothing but tips, points and coulters and dreams of tillage trains, subsoilers and power harrows; the longer the weather stays open and dry, the more he longs to plunge into virgin soil and sow seed.

One school of pub thought, led, naturally, by horrible Old Eli, is that it is all Freudian and nothing that a week's wet weather will not cure. The other is that Real Farmer is terrified to admit he has had nothing to do since the middle of October – and that is the view I take.

It is not so bad for the Quiche Farmers. They have all gone shooting and their wives are so exhausted from their thrice-weekly aerobics that they object only feebly.

But the Real . . . oh it is terrible what's happened to the Real.

There's a Real Man I know who normally spends November happily up to his knees in mud with a massive chain on his draw-bar, pulling himself out of the peculiarly glutinous clay which he pleases to call his seed-bed.

There's another who usually celebrates 1 November by removing the top eighteen inches of rotting, black silage from the front few feet of his clamp.

Last week I saw them both, shirt collars rubbing and shoes

too tight, herded into the front of the Rover, heading for a day's shopping not a thousand miles from Sloane Street.

Consider the shame – and expense – of it; and the ignominy of failing to find a single agricultural excuse that would stand up to their wives' cajolings.

There is worse to come. I am told by an impeccably reliable source that Farmer X has spent a whole week in the garden. (I shall not name him for he is a man of some standing in the community and my revelations would certainly disqualify him from ever holding NFU office again.)

'It was either that or Lanzarote,' he mumbled in pathetic self-defence when openly accused of this at the market last week. What a terrible admission; but is it any wonder he is so subdued, trimming hedges while his two 100-horse-power beasts stand silent in the yard?

There is a bright side however. When the mildew takes over the September-drilled barley and the wheat takes up the pre-emergence weed-killer and dies, there are, this year, saving graces.

We can all stop chopping logs, sweeping leaves and shopping, climb back on our tractors and look busy again.

Time to Unwind

The tyres are coming off the silage clamps all over Britain and the rhythm of the seasons, which stays the same from century to century, means it is once again time for the farmer to unwind, put behind him the sweat and toil of harvest and seed-time and enjoy those simple rural traditions which are the very heart and lungs of this great country of ours.

Dynasty, the NFU branch AGM, discussion groups, fast pheasants, slow horses, skittles, an attempt on the new Chinese restaurant, a trip to town, and before you know it, it is time for *Dynasty* again.

Such pleasures are the stuff and fibre of Britain's long, dark country evenings, the good thick blood which pumps through the arteries of the great estates and the veins of the lonely farmhouses, the staff of life through the hard northern winter and . . .

Mr Scargill tells us that this is two countries, divided by class, and I am well aware that agriculturally we are two nations . . . those who have finished drilling and those who haven't. Come

to think of it, there's a third nation – those who have not yet finished combining.

Leader of this third group is an hospitable friend in Worcestershire who last week was still poised to harvest his evening primrose crop. They do say, in Worcestershire, 'Primrose be best when 'er's 'ad a good 'ard frost on 'er.'

And there is something very macho about scraping the frost off the combine cab glass before firing up.

On second thoughts, perhaps we are two nations split between those who milk cows and those who do not. For the former, anxiously waiting to hear whether the quota board will graciously allow an extra half cow, unwinding is still out of the question.

Then again, perhaps the split is geographical, east against west. Gathered round the slurry pits of the west they say that on the great shoots of East Anglia they talk of little other than the difficulty of finding a spare bed in Barbados in January.

So let me start again: for a few fortunate farmers it is the season to unwind, to lift eyes from the day-to-day grind of eking a living from the soil and consider once again the wider world beyond the slatted shed.

Different farmers unwind in different ways. Nothing shows the contrast between the quiche and the real half of the farming nation better than shooting. Quiche shoots are Range Rovers, keepers, Barbours bought at Badminton, lunch in two groups (Mr Scargill's two nations?), VSOP. Real shoots are spaniels, over and unders, leggings, roots and beer.

(Incidentally, a perceptive Shropshire reader gave me this excellent quiche definition: the Quiche Farmer works during the week and has weekends free; the Real Farmer works right through every weekend because he is so busy Monday to Friday attending farm sales and market.)

Like hibernating animals, farmers know the importance of conserving energy through the winter months, hoarding food and fuel and lying doggo until the spring.

Only meetings lure them abroad. Drawn by the promise of stimulating company and draught beer, they leave their firesides for an hour or two but scurry back nervously ere long, drawn by the grey glow of the television, the amber gleam of the Scotch bottle, the relentless need to feed the hungry Aga/Rayburn/Jøtul/Scanfield.

Peace creeps over rural Britain. Politicians' strident voices fade into the distance and the din of conservationists is muted. The last trespassers are gathering on telephone wires, the litter-leavers head for their suburban breeding grounds. In manor house and simple cott . . .

Old Eli Has His Say

WE MAKE THE ACQUAINTANCE OF A MISERABLE
OLD WISEACRE WHO INFESTS THE PUBLIC BAR
OF THE LOCAL TAVERN

Coming Out in Euroflushes

This here Euro-election is bringing all of us round these parts out in hot Euroflushes of excitement, and I suppose it must be the same all over the country.

People in the local are talking of little else, and I fear that the polling stations will be so busy next Thursday that they'll have to bring in the Pony Club to control the crowds.

We are all that keen, you see, to make our mark on history by voting in the first international election in the history of the world. After all, it's not often you get the chance to make a mark on history, no matter how many scars history may have left on you. A chance to get your own back, kind of thing.

What's more, it's an election which we farmers can really get our teeth stuck into, what with the Common Agricultural Policy being the biggest thing to have come out of the whole boiling pot.

To give you an idea of how thrilled we all are, the shove ha'penny down the local has been completely abandoned, and all the regulars have been playing Euroquizzes – a bit of a cross between University Challenge and Mastermind. Old Ted does a lovely Bamber Gascoigne and George's Magnus Magnusson is quite the best in the area.

Thought you might like to see some of the questions which were asked, just to give you a feel of the way things go on and an idea of the standard of the contest. I think you'll see how Euroexciting it all is – better than shove pfennig, anyway.

'Right, this evening's contestants are the team from the Old Bull – Le Vieux Taureau – *and the boys from the Pig and Whistle* – Il Maiale e il Fischio.*'

'Old Bull, it's your starter for ten. What percentage of the Italian sheep flock is to be found in Sardinia?'

'Thirty per cent.'

'Correct . . . What is the official definition of Grade 2a Vitelloni bulls in Italian slaughterhouses?'

'Those not classified as Grade 1.'

'Correct.'

You can see how this kind of quick-fire wit keeps us on the edge of our seats.

'What's this week's pig price at Rungis?' . . . 'Give me the annual throughput in tonnes of Frankfurt abattoirs' . . . 'What are the current Special Weighing Coefficients in Florence?' . . . 'Explain the difference between MCAs and TCAs' . . . 'What is a currency basket?' . . . '. . . 'A variable levy?' . . . 'A sluicegate price?' . . . 'The best bar in the vicinity of Ganly's Market, Dublin?'

Every Agri-Euro-subject you can think of comes up for discussion. Only last week, Old Eli chose Greek olive oil production as his special subject, and very well he did too; and Greece not even a full member. The Saloon trade was very impressed.

'Course it's not without its funny side. Like when Geoff said there were 50,000 people employed by the Community when everyone in the whole pub knew it were no more than 15,000. Or when Harry said there were £9,131,743,000 in the Community budget to be spent on agriculture when really, of course, the answer is 9,131, 743,000 EUAs. Or when Fred thought the Lomé Convention had something to do with getting a good tilth;

and Alf thought the ACP countries were All Conservative Politically.

Oh, we do have some good laughs. Haven't seen the shove-lira board for Eurodays.

I suppose that after 7 June all the excitement will pass and we shall be back to talking about our old topics – monetarist policies in nineteenth-century Europe, Wittgenstein's role in the development of logical positivism, Pat Eddery's chances of being champion jockey, and so on. But somehow, once we've made our mark on history, I don't think things down here will ever be quite the same again.

Doreen's youngest is being christened Helmut on Saturday, Albert seems to prefer Pernod to his usual pint of sludge, and I have heard talk of a shove-centime league. I wonder if you can shove a EUA.

You Can't Beat a Moorhen for Rabbiting

Yesterday several of us were out rabbiting, for the pests are worse around here than they have been for years – possibly because we are almost in sight of Watership Down and all the favourable publicity has gone to the animals' fool heads.

We stopped for a pub lunch and talk turned to the wonders of nature in general and the miracle of the moorhen in particular.

One of our number is a founder member of the moorhen fan club. He reckons it is the most remarkable of all the birds because of its extraordinary versatility. It swims, he says, underwater like a frog; travels so fast on the surface that it makes a duck look clumsy; puts many animals to shame with its skill in running on dry land; flies higher and straighter when driven than some hand-reared pheasants.

Just about the only thing it cannot do is climb trees or sit up and beg, and no doubt Barbara Woodhouse could put the latter right in a trice.

Old Eli, who was quietly supping in the corner, overheard our conversation, and could not resist adding his two ha'pence worth.

'What you needs is a moorhen for your rabbiting,' he said. 'Good moorhen puts ferrets in the shade when it comes to rabbiting.'

Silence.

Even the great moorhen fancier himself looked puzzled at this one.

Eli explained: 'My grandad used to keep a couple o' moorhens for putting down rabbit holes just like you would a ferret. Trouble was, all the rabbits round us had got used to grandad's ol' ferrets, so he said: "What they needs is a bit of a shock," and he started trying various birds down the burries.

'Coots worked well for a time, but grandad reckoned the rabbits saw their white heads too quick and got too much warning. Chickens was too fat, and one grew to like it down below and started laying underground and grandad didn't fancy mining for eggs. Eventually it became obvious you couldn't beat a moorhen for the job. Tough little creatures they are. Grandad used to say it were their underwater training; like the SAS.'

Silence again, broken by the moorhen fan. 'There you are,' he said. 'They are the most remarkable bird of all. Eli has proved the point.'

'Ah, but they did have one trouble,' drawled the old man, reaching out his glass for a refill. 'In the deeper holes they didn't seem to like the dark. Lost their bearings, sort of. But grandad soon sorted that out.'

We all strained forward to learn the secret of how to stop a moorhen being afraid of the dark.

'He used to save a candle end and mount it on the back of a

tortoise. Then he lit the candle and put the tortoise down the hole ahead of the moorhen. Hedgehogs don't work because although 'tis easier to make the candle stay upright, the hot wax runs down and burns 'em. Tortoises is the chaps for the job. Does for the moorhen what the pillar of flame did for Moses.'

I don't think any of us believed the tortoise bit of the story, but we did spend a damp half hour after lunch trying to catch a moorhen so that we could put Eli's tale to the test at the mouth of the nearest rabbit hole.

Moorhens are hard to catch, and we were still splashing around in the stream at closing time when Eli came out of the pub and climbed on his bicycle.

'Here, Eli, how did your grandad catch the moorhens in the first place?'

'Ah, well, to catch a moorhen when she's swimming, what you need is a good hungry pike . . .' the old man called over his shoulder, smiling, and his legs started to pedal slowly up and down as he cycled enigmatically out of earshot.

First Steps on the Farming Ladder

Old Eli reckons he's got the answer to this here farming ladder, or lack of it. Mind you, he got the wrong end of the stick at first, but now he says he's got the thing just about sorted out and the NFU and CLA blokes may as well relax.

It all started when somebody in the bar of the Happy Heifer started on about the dismal prospect for young farmers. Young Straightfurrow-Keene, I think it was, home from Cirencester for the week-end. Funny he should bring the subject up, seeing as how his prospects mostly revolve around his Dad's thousand acres, but that's beside the point.

Eli didn't understand about the ladder at first. Logically enough, he kept seeing it as a thing you go down, not up. So when Straightfurrow-Keene kept on about 'staying on the farming ladder', he chimed in: 'Don't see how you can fall off when you're starting with a thousand acres, and most of 'em in wheat. Don't see many rotten rungs there. Leastways, not 'less the pheasants drives you out,' and he gave one of his foulest slurps as he buried his mouth in his beer.

Patiently we explained to him about the breakdown of the landlord-tenant system, and painted graphic pictures of the hundreds of youngsters pouring out of agricultural colleges who could never hope to farm for themselves; and although he muttered something about how he thought they all wanted to be pop stars, he did shut up for the rest of the evening.

Now the trouble is that since he gave up milking, he's got too much time on his hands, and he's very much taken to reading the newspapers from cover to cover. The only thing he never reads about is farming.

Last week he came up with his great plan – well, several great plans.

'First step on your farming ladder,' he said, 'is to get into they gold futures.'

'Eli,' someone said. 'You're ignorant. The gold price fell $100 an ounce at the end of February. You'd have been wiped out.'

'Right,' snapped back the old beggar. 'That's why I says get in now. She'll never be lower. She's at $400 now. She'll be $4,000 in 1985,' and he hawked his throat in a noise that once sent shivers round the ring at the local mart.

'That's your first step on your ladder,' he said. 'And when you've made your pile, get out and buy land.

'Or here's another first step. They explorers all gets famous, and once you're famous you just signs up with that Mark McCormack and you're rich. You wants to be the first man to roller-skate to the North Pole; or cross Brixton on foot; or announce publicly that you can't stand Frank Sinatra. If you lives to tell the tale, you've got it made.'

Most of us were backing away from his corner by now, trying to get out of range, but he was just warming to his theme.

'Horses is another way in,' he said. 'I done an each-way treble at Fontwell in 1949 as would have bought me fifty acres easy. Trouble was my fancy in the last race didn't finish 'til early 1950 . . . but 'tis the principle of the thing, the principle.

'And look at that McEnroe; he's got the answer. Or they redundant executives wi' them golden 'andshakes. They'll all be into the farming ladder soon enough. Or they Lloyds blokes there was all the fuss about. Oh there's a million ways o' getting your foot on the first rung, most of them marked out by pound signs. Well, all of 'em actually.'

When Straightfurrow-Keene was told of Eli's theory, he hurried back to college, bowled over by the wisdom of it all. Now the place is running lectures on commodities, racehorses, pro tennis, and redundancy negotiations, all under the heading 'Acquiring a holding'.

They even sent a lecturer to question Old Eli about his theories.

'There's a large element of chance in all these schemes,' he pointed out.

''Course,' said Eli. 'You're meant to be educating them for agriculture, aren't you?'

Keep it in the Family

With polling day little more than a week away, County Council election fever is mounting to a frenzied climax. In pubs around the country, the cut and thrust of political debate has pushed even Torvill and Dean to the sidelines of conversation.

Naturally, the crowd in the Happy Heifer is no exception. The other evening we were bemoaning the way in which, willy-nilly, we all get carried along once every four years by the kind of political hysteria seldom seen outside a Republican convention hall.

'Answer to that seems pretty simple,' said Old Eli after one of his long, introspective silences. 'Make 'em 'ereditary.'

None of us has ever been able to tie a neat label on Old Eli's politics – he passionately supports both Stafford Cripps and Enoch Powell – but this addition to his Collected Thoughts and Wisdom stunned us all.

Like many of his ideas, however, the more we turned it over, the more we liked it. It would, indeed, do away with all the election nonsense, but elections are not the biggest evil in local government.

That award goes to party politics; and in time, we thought, Eli's brainchild would purge county politics of the party whip, of budding professional politicians who use the council committee rooms as steps towards Westminster, of councillors whose loyalties to Downing Street and the Department of the Environment are stronger than their links with their division's parish halls.

Old Eli's vision was of a return to the turn of the century when *noblesse* obliged benevolent squires to give their time to local affairs.

'Ha,' we chorused, quick to spot the weakness in the old boy's scheme. 'Not much *noblesse* around nowadays.'

How, then, to select the families to which we were prepared to entrust our rate precept for ever more? As always in the

Heifer, we arrived at our answers through steady and logical reasoning.

First, we halved the number of councillors, doubled the size of their divisions and paid them all £50 a day attendance allowance. Once every generation, every family will have to be re-elected by its constituents – a combination of democracy and inheritance.

We took the four main responsibilities of the County Council and settled what sort and condition of person would be best equipped to handle them. Environment – roads, strategic planning, footpaths, mineral workings – was the easiest to settle. Farmers and farmers' wives were the only group with the specialist knowledge required.

Education, on the other hand, requires no specialist knowledge, just the ability to control striking teachers and other dissidents. We could not think of anyone better equipped to display common sense and firm management than . . . farmers and their wives.

It is always difficult to find anyone prepared to take on the worries of the social services committee with its wide range of human problems and permanent shortage of money. We racked our brains to come up with the kind of person used to managing on a shoe-string. Eventually, it dawned on us that the solution was staring us in the face: farmers' wives and their husbands.

After that, the fourth major committee, public protection, was a doddle. Public protection means running the fire brigade; all the world knows that the biggest fire risk and nuisance since the Blitz is straw and stubble burning, so it seems only logical that those responsible for starting the conflagrations should be charged with extinguishing them.

And Why is the Combine Moving Much Slower than Ben Johnson?

'It's amazing,' said Old Eli. 'Them boys in Rome can do 100 metres in nine point something seconds, while this old combine does five metres in the same time if she's lucky.'

Eli has come out of retirement to help cart the corn and this year for the first time in his long life he has a radio on the tractor.

Of course he does not approve of the thing. 'Never needed no wireless on the old Fergie,' he said when first he climbed aboard and opened up the windscreen, side windows, roof, and rear windows of the Q Cab.

'Not safe, these cabs,' he muttered, as he always does, 'can't hear what's goin' on about you,' and we had great trouble persuading him not to spend fifteen minutes removing the doors.

Early in the afternoon he was parked at the top of the field waiting for a load and I was surprised to see that the cab was again hermetically sealed.

'Had to shut the windows,' he explained. 'That combine makes such a racket, I can't hear Woman's Hour.'

Now his evening conversation in the bar of the Happy Heifer has come to sound like readings from a radio critic's diary, spiced with slivers of arcane fact and controversial opinion lifted straight from Radio Two or Four . . . the Light Programme and the Home Service, he calls them.

The other day he had over-dosed badly on Henry Blofeld. 'Listen Old Thing,' he said to me. 'The trouble with Woman's Hour is that it is too gynaecological. It comes too soon after dinner for all that talk about tubes and canals. You would think a woman's insides was private, but they talks about them as if they was planning a public transport system.'

Another day he spent half an hour with Radio Four getting up to date on the situation in Iran. I suppose it is fair to say that the grasp of international affairs maintained by the Heifer's regulars is based more on prejudice than knowledge, but Eli's analysis of the difference between Sunnis and Shias ('them Sunnis folds their hand when they prays; Shias don't'), and the role of Hojetoleslam Rafsanjani *vis-à-vis* Khomeini, was too expert for most of us.

So too was the information that he had been listening to a Canadian scientist who spends his life collecting rats' breath and chemically analysing it, all in the good cause of creating a rat bait that the rodents will find irresistible.

From the Daily Service to the Archers, Eli is becoming a Radio Four bore, but there has been plenty of sport around to suck him into Radio Two occasionally and news from the Olympic Stadium in Rome has been reaching the harvest field miraculously fast. The whole operation stopped so that everyone could listen to the final of the 800 metres, which says something about our sense of priorities.

And why is the combine moving so much slower than Ben Johnson? As Eli correctly diagnosed, it's the wild oats. They have never been worse. Last year I thought that season after season of spraying was beginning to pay dividends as an increasing number of fields seemed to be clean, and I must have lowered my guard because this year they have come powering in like Lloyd Honeyghan (Radio Two, 8.20) and taken over areas that I felt were free of the weed.

One field was so bad we desiccated it. That helped a little but the oats were so tangled and matted that the spray only reached the top layer.

Old Eli climbed down from his tractor to help me pull another thick, damp wedge of the beastly things from between the combine's clenched front teeth.

'In the time it takes to do this, Aouita could run from here to the Heifer and back,' he said. Sometimes you could cheerfully throttle the old sod.

The Farmer Imitates The Thrusting Executive

IN WHICH IT IS DEMONSTRATED THAT THE QUALITY
OF WHICH A FARMER STANDS MOST IN NEED IS THAT
OF RESOLUTE DECISIVENESS

How to Sell Seed with a Swing . . .

Conversation overheard last week, in a farmyard, in the rain, somewhere in England. The names have been changed to protect the innocent.

'How do you do? My name is John Hard-Sell, I am the new representative in these parts for Tonsofgrain Seeds. Just moved down here from the Mull of Kintyre, where my company has had tremendous success with its new winter wheat varieties. I expect you have read about it.'

'*Well, no, I buy my seed from the local merchant and I have no complaints.*'

'Oh, yes, some of these little merchants are excellent in their way, but the trouble is they just cannot get the new varieties, and of course first-generation seed can only be bought from us, so if you want to grow for seed . . .'

'*I am not really interested in first-generation seed. I am not set up to grow seed corn and I have no clean fields to plough this year anyway.*'

'What about this meadow here?'

'*That's the lawn.*'

'Yes of course, I see it now. When you come to consider reseeding it, Tonsofgrain Grass Seed Division has recently introduced some new mixtures that grow particularly slowly and are specially intended to reduce the number of times per season that a lawn needs cutting.'

'*I shan't be reseeding it. I find that plenty of moss keeps it green and needs little cutting.*'

'Fine. Can we return to the question of winter wheat for next season?'

'*Look, I haven't even thought about it. We haven't got the spring barley in the ground yet; it will be weeks before I start to think about winter wheat.*'

'How would it be if I just put you down for some Fiasco with no obligation on your part; it is bound to be in short supply, and I would like to think you were covered if you did decide you needed it. Fiasco is our new variety with exceptionally high shedding resistance.'

'*No, really, you're very kind but I am perfectly happy with the seed I get from my local merchants.*'

'Well, look, I'll tell you what. As part of our service we will come and do a few soil tests in your arable fields, and if conditions seem right for Fiasco, I'll put your name down for some. No obligation. It will cost you nothing. We'll confirm later. What can you lose?'

'*My local people have always proved quite satisfactory before, and I never order before September from them.*'

'Right. Yes. No way am I knocking them. But we find these small firms are often slow to jump on the bandwagon . . . I mean keep abreast of the latest exciting developments in the trade . . .'

'*No, really, it is not worth thinking about.*'

'I quite understand. If you are not interested in Fiasco I am sure Futility will appeal. As you will see from the leaflet, this is the kind of wheat that will drive Huntsman right off the market. It is specially designed with a weak area on the north side of the straw so that when it lodges, it all falls in the same direction. So long as you are always heading south on the combine, it is amazingly easy to pick up.

'Added to that, there are no diseases against which it cannot be sprayed. Now I cannot tell you what seed Futility will cost next season, so I think it would be best if I just have some put aside for you . . . with no obligation of course . . . and in a month or so I shall come to you and confirm. I am putting your name on this order form, but of course it commits you to nothing.'

'Well . . .'

'No, no. It just means that if you do confirm you will qualify for our early order offer. You will receive a free copy of *How to Succeed in the Grain Business*, a metrication chart and the chance to win a twelfth share in a two-year-old in training near Newmarket.

'Thank you. Goodbye. See you soon.'

Adapting to a Happy Family Farm

Did you read the reports of why British workers find it difficult to adapt to life in Japanese-owned 'happy family' factories? Prof. H. Inohara of Tokyo has been over here to carry out a socio-economic survey of life in British subsidiaries of Japanese industrial companies and he went away exasperated by our reluctance to wear a uniform or switch jobs.

Less well publicized was Mr Inohara's study of the only Japanese-run 'happy family' farm in Britain. He reports:

'The day starts at 7.30 am with calisthenics for workers and management alike. Attendance at these exercises is poor. Various sicknesses are used as excuses for late arrival, principally "hangovers" and "broken alarms".

'Dress is also highly irregular. The workers favour torn denims and faded donkey jackets and often refuse to wear the magenta overalls provided by the company. They seem oblivious to the fact that family spirit is greatly enhanced by fifteen minutes of synchronized movement, performed as a team by men in matching uniforms. Company wellies are well used, however, and company string vests seem popular.

'Many of the slogans and notices posted around the yards and barns by the company have been removed. These urged workers to LOVE THE TRACTOR and STRIVE FOR HIGHER GROSS MARGINS but in many instances have been replaced with obscure messages such as UNITED RULE, JOE

JORDAN FOR PRIME MINISTER and TED, GONE FOR
A PINT, BACK LATER – ALF.

'It must be remembered that slogans are posted to keep the
workers' thoughts on his job and off domestic and leisure time
activities.

'After calisthenics, the men go about their tasks. All tractors
and buildings are fitted with radios through which the company
song is broadcast once an hour, giving employees the opportunity to join in the rousing company chorus:

We love our rain, we love our mud; we even love our slurry.
We love the flap at harvest time; we love the autumn hurry.
We sing if we repair machines.
We smile if cows abort,
Because we go about our tasks content in this one thought –
Our farm is great; our boss is grand;
Happy in the muck we stand.

'Sadly, many employees are not grasping this opportunity to
show their contentment and comradeship and instead leave their
radios tuned to a subversive influence called "Terry Wogan"
who appears to condone idleness and time-wasting.

'Half-way through the morning, all work stops for the tea
ceremony. This is particularly interesting because the bad old
customs of British management have been blended with the
traditional Japanese ritual to produce a happening unique to
our happy family farm.

'Leaning back in their tractor seats, the men ceremonially
unscrew the tops of their "vacuum flasks" and delicately pour a
sweet, steaming, amber liquid into brightly coloured cups.

'Some eat cake, biscuits or "jam butties" while sipping this
infusion. All over the farm it is a time for quiet reflection and
contemplation. The workers are at one with nature. They draw
their inspiration from the rocks, flowers and blossoms around.

'English fields are rich in "wild oats", "thistles", "nettles" and
other fragile plants which the men contemplate during "tea
break".

'The company has wisely issued all employees with cards
which the men can read while they rest, listing production
targets, yield figures, fertilizer prices and other statistics essential to a proper understanding of the work.

'I was pleased to see that these cards are treated with proper
reverence. They are often wrapped in newspapers to protect
them from dirt and the elements and are referred to while still
concealed in the inner pages of journals such as *The Sun*.

'In conclusion, I recommend that the happy family farm be continued; but that the parent company must be firmer with its child employees.'

Is There a Computer to Make Micro Decisions?

It is like the old stand-up comic's joke: 'I say, I say, my wife and I have a perfect arrangement. I take the big decisions, such as whether or not the Americans should be involved in the Lebanon, whether the Liberal Party should amalgamate with the SDP, and if Robson is right to keep Wilkins in midfield. And I let the wife take the small ones, like whether we should move house or buy a new car.'

I know there are plenty of machines around waiting to rap out answers to the big problems. Input them with all the variables between the lifestyles of merchant bankers and farmers and their bossy little screens will immediately glow with advice on which career you should have chosen.

But what I want to know is whether I should roll this field before discing that one.

Program the beast with your fertilizer, spray, seed, diesel, and manpower requirements, the cost of replacement ploughshares and your yield per acre and it will pause only a fraction of a second before smugly telling you to try gravel extraction or a wild-life park. But ask it whether it is worth starting to drill twenty acres at 4.00 pm when there's a big black rain squall coming in from the west, and it will stare mutely back at you.

The small, dozen-a-day decisions are important for two reasons. You can get in a serious muddle if you get enough of them wrong; and you might be getting them wrong all the time without realizing it.

An example of the first is the kind of exam-paper conundrum which you face all the time: 'You have two tractors at your disposal, one at point A, the other at point B. The harrows, roller, seed and wheel-cages are at point C. You want to drill Field D.

'What is the minimum number of tractor movements required to get the implements to the field and get you home for tea (point E)?'

You have only got to make a small error in a situation like that and an afternoon can slip by without anything being achieved other than a five-mile walk.

I imagine a computer could tackle that sort of problem; the trouble is it would be at point F, wouldn't it?

The thought that I might be set in a routine of poor decisions without realizing it is a nagging worry.

Once when I was young and callow I sat in a punt with friends at Henley Regatta watching a man in a neighbouring boat topping his strawberries while gazing at the racing and the crowds. One by one he selected a strawberry without looking at it, took off its top, dropped the strawberry into the river and carefully put the green stalk into his bowl. I am ashamed to say that none of us warned him of his mistake, so keen were we to see the expression on his face when he came to add the cream and sugar.

Am I on the way to a plateful of greenery? Are all my strawberries drifting away downstream? Would anybody tell me if they were?

This year, for the first time, for instance, I ..m putting no nitrogen in with the winter corn. I now learn that most people round here gave up the autumn N years ago, but nobody told me and season after season I have bought more costly fertilizer than I needed.

Perhaps there is also a computer which would have saved me that. But would I ever have asked it the right question?

Got to go now. I must help sheet up the wool; or fit the subsoiler legs; or load the seed wheat, or move the cattle. Oh for a microchip to tell me which needs doing most urgently.

I don't know, though. It is much more friendly being told by the wife.

Caught Out by Drought?

Did the cold spell catch you out? Was your tow-rope broken, anti-freeze inadequate, diesel waxy?

And what about clothing? Did she turn your veteran long johns into dusters during the summer and consign that woolly hat to the WI stall?

Do you mean to say you do not follow the Automobile Association's advice and always park the Land Rover with its bonnet down wind to keep rain and snow off the engine, cover the windscreen with polythene and wipe it with meths, plug the lock with an 'ice key' (whatever that may be), charge the battery once a week, put a blanket under the bonnet and a sheet over the radiator?

Did you not equip it with torch, blanket, extra clothes, gloves, jump leads, warning triangles, spade, sand, salt, a supply of food, several thermos flasks, an Agatha Christie, marker flares and a transistor radio?

Before the snow you surrounded the Jøtul with logs, the Aga with Polish coal, and primed the stand-by generator, did you not?

All your troughs are properly lagged, aren't they? You have a spare bulk tank for the day the tanker can't get down the road, don't you? The hay is near the sheep, isn't it? And you ordered the extra cake well in advance so there is no chance of running low on that, I know you did.

Above all, throughout the freeze, you have obeyed medical advice and shunned all spirits which, of course, lower the body temperature and send your blood towards the skin surface, accelerating heat loss. Yes, I've noticed, the whisky bottle has not been touched since Christmas.

So far, so good, but January is not over yet, and twelve years' intensive research by the young and enthusiastic team at the National Organic Couch Grass and Regular Fibre Unit reveals that before very long – certainly within the next six months – there is an eighty-two per cent chance of a MAJOR HEAT-WAVE AND DROUGHT.

NOW is the time when the far-sighted farmer gets ready for those fearful summer days when day after day of relentless sun bakes Britain brown.

Many chemists can be persuaded to give discounts at this time of year on sun-tan oil, dark glasses and salt tablets. Wise agriculturalists looking for expenditure before the end of the financial year take advantage of these low winter prices. Why don't you?

At the same time, the January sales are the ideal opportunity to stock your wardrobe with shorts, light cotton shirts and sandals (the whisper from the fashion buyers at Smithfield was that the open-toe look will be all the rage by harvest time).

Don't forget, as you get older and lose your hair, more and more of your head will be susceptible to sun-burn so buy a sun hat or solar topee now and have it handy for the heatwave.

Caught out by drought last year? Don't let it happen again. Workers at the Sabbatical Institute of Social and Environmental Research and Countryside Resource Centre have revived the old ice-house principle on a massive scale. They advise: 'Get in a

JCB, dig a hole about fifty metres into the side of the nearest hill, fill it with ice and snow and block the entrance.

'Come July, progressively expose the contents to the sun and the melting snows will provide enough water to keep three sheep for a week. EEC grants are available.'

Incidentally, don't forget that Met Office records suggest that it might rain one day. Now is the time to stock up on those hard-to-get wellies and waterproof jackets; did you know that on many market stalls and street corners umbrellas cost less in January than when it is raining? The well-organized farmer . . .

Win
Win
Win

It has been obvious for some time that I needed to take the Agricultural Training Board's 'negotiation skills' course. My negotiation skills are so fearsome that last summer, when we were on holiday in Turkey, I traded ten packets of cigarettes for a sponge when the fisherman selling the sponge had opened the bargaining at seven packets.

It took me five difficult minutes to beat him up to ten.

So off I went to the 'negotiation skills' day. It was instructive and useful and I enjoyed myself, but I do not think I shall drive harder bargains as a result of it.

I suppose there are two categories of farmer who sign up for the course. The first is the kind of intractable businessman who finds it hard to strike a deal because he hates to lose face, to budge from his stated position, to reduce his price or up his offer.

The second is the kind who ends up with a deal but usually feels that he has got the worst of it.

Perhaps the ATB should run two different negotiation skills courses, one for the stubborn who need to learn to be more flexible and one for those who need to be toughened up because they are already so flexible that they bend over backwards to touch their toes.

The course I took seemed to be designed for the first category. We were told to adopt something called a 'win-win philosophy' which means that both sides in a negotiation should finish it thinking they have won. All day the emphasis was on compromise. 'Try to reach an agreement acceptable to both of you . . . seek to maintain and develop good relations in the longer term,' we were told.

I was surprised by this approach. If I have been haggling over the discount on a new tractor, do I want the supplier to think he has won when we shake hands on the deal? When the gipsy comes round to buy the scrap metal, do I want him to drive away with a loaded lorry and a grin on his face yet again?

I went on the course hoping to be made meaner and nastier. I have got plenty of 'longer-term good relations'. What I want are some short-term cash discounts, prices cut to the bone, sponge fishermen in awe of my persuasiveness and strength.

I came away from the day feeling that, instead of a course run by two rather nice chaps in Wantage Civic Centre, I should have gone on a five-day seminar run by gentlemen with Italian names and loud suits above a pool hall in Chicago.

I floated this theory over an American acquaintance who uses Concorde like you and I use a Land Rover and negotiates oil by the thousand barrels with Arabs, Texans and Chinese.

'Have you got where you are today by adopting a win-win philosophy?' I asked him. 'How are your longer-term relationships? At business school in the States, were you taught the value of compromise above all?'

He smiled. 'In my language the only good negotiation is one where you have screwed the other guy into the ground and left him for dead. There is nothing personal in it. He will respect you for doing a good job and treat you carefully the next time you do business together. There can be only one winner in a negotiation. Just make sure it's you.'

I believe the American approach is right. Compromises do not make both parties happy; they are much more likely to leave both dissatisfied.

The Paper Mountain Grows

IT BECOMES APPARENT THAT OUR FREE-SPIRITED
HERO IS NOT WORKING FOR HIMSELF

Forms of Control . . .

It's not such a bad life as a civil servant. Look at it this way: the days we spend working for the Government are no worse than those we spend working for those bastions of the free market system – the banks and mortgage companies.

The trick is to count the blessings: although our income is state-controlled and much of our lives state-organized, at least we have not yet been formally nationalized. Only if Mr Kinnock considers agriculture to be one of the 'commanding heights of the economy' when he is in power will that happen.

So lie back and enjoy it. Although this is by no means the high season for forms and claims, the last few weeks have seen the state exercising tight control over the farm.

First there was the compulsory September dipping which kept the drill out of action for a day. The only sheep which leave here in the normal course of events go straight to the slaughterhouse, we have never had sheep scab in the area, we carry out the normal summer dip conscientiously.

Why then pull us away from the vital autumn arable work to dip the sheep – all six weeks in lamb, incidentally, although the vet says they will not suffer?

Then there was the request from the Department of the Environment. One of my trees fell into the grounds of the local public monument – to wit, one castle – crushing the state-owned chain-link fence. Would we please get on and repair it?

Admittedly the accident happened last winter, but the fence serves no useful purpose and there always seem to be more important things to do – such as complying with the County Council's letter requesting that we fell four trees overhanging the state-run road.

The temptation here is to let them fall, for I have noticed that small trees which fall in an area easily approached by car, mysteriously and quickly disappear towards one of the local wood-burners . . . but I suppose we must comply. It would be embarrassing if one of them fell into a car before being sawn up.

The Department of the Environment has just fired its second barrel in the form of a notice about historic buildings – to wit, one bridge.

'For the purpose of enabling the Secretary of State blah blah blah' . . . twenty-seven lines, three paragraphs, one sub-paragraph and six sub-sub-paragraphs, full of 'as the case may be' and 'as may be so specified' all of which combine to tell me that I shall be fined £100 if I don't tell them who owns the bridge and for what it is used.

Any 'misstatement . . . imprisonment for a term not exceeding two years . . .'

I find it all so frightening.

Perhaps they will lump the fine together with the one I may incur as a consequence of the District Council proceeding against me for failing to plough in ash within thirty-six hours of burning stubble 'without a reasonable excuse'.

Do you think it would be reasonable to say I was busy filling in my VAT return? ('Failure to make a return is an offence punishable by up to . . .') It is high time that every local authority had its own satellite or U2 system for surveillance of the cringeing ratepayers. How do we expect the poor overworked environmental officers to know what we are using our bridges for, whether we are sawing down our trees, if we are burning at a weekend, when we dip our sheep and how valid are our snivelling little excuses?

. . . *and Torture*

June is the month of the long forms. Like dinosaur bones disappearing beneath centuries of glacial waste, the census and the three FHDS forms lie peacefully in the in-tray while succeeding strata of invoices and VAT returns accrete above them.

When finally you haul the fossils out, do not succumb to the temptation to write facetious remarks all over them.

I have to face this urge every year. It was sown in me when I was a child on a flight to France with a grand and upright friend of my grandparents. To my surprise, when the little immigration card was handed to him by the stewardess, he filled it in with fiction – a made-up passport number, 'Place of birth: Timbuk-too' and signed it 'Charlie Chaplin'.

When passport control inspected his card, I stood timorously behind waiting for him to be whisked away to the Bastille, but he was waved through regardless.

I have never yet dared treat forms in such a cavalier fashion. All those preliminaries about the Agricultural Statistics Act 1979 (as amended by the Agriculture (Amendment) Act 1984) sound to me like Holy Writ. 'Penalties may be imposed on any person who . . . recklessly gives false information.'

What penalties? A century or two in purgatory? A week on the rack in the Ministry basement? A lifetime shunted from one work camp to another of the Whitehall Archipelago?

I long 'recklessly and without reasonable excuse' to give false information but I chicken out. (That's chicken as in questions 125/126: 'Fowls for breeding'.)

Take: 'Land Given Up: f. Other reasons for decrease in area.' The temptation to run amok here is like a carrot patch to a rabbit. 'Let ten acres go because I was too busy filling in forms to farm them.' 'Built shed for files on half an acre.' 'Built rest home for exhausted desk-top calculators on .0003478 hectares.'

Why does MAFF have this prurient interest in ages and weights? To what strange obsession are we pandering when we separate our female cattle more than two years old from those one year old and under two. Why does it matter whether bulls are for service or not? Is the Ministry guilty of ageism and sexism? Is there no Council for Weightist Equality which will

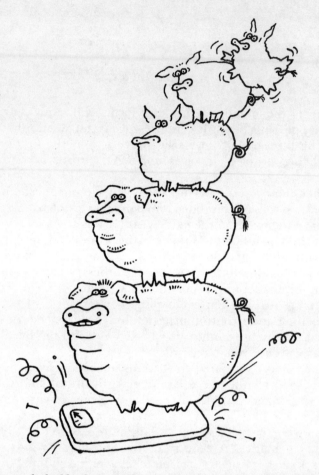

protest on behalf of the pigs who are split into five different weight groups?

There is more discrimination a dozen questions further on where guinea fowl are specifically excluded from the 'poussins and other table fowl' category. Where do I list my guinea fowl and why can I not include game birds?

An interesting innovation this year is the 'Terms of Occupancy' section which starts with the grammatically doubtful remark 'Area owned: this is where the land is not let to you. You are not a tenant.'

I have written: 'The land belongs to the people; this question reflects the kind of outdated adherence to exhausted capitalist dogma which we have come to expect from the Fascist Thatcher State. Power to the regular whole-time hired workers (see notes 57–64).' But I expect I shall cross it out again.

Cheque Writer's Cramp

Here are the month's invoices, waiting to be paid, beside them is the chequebook, open and inviting, there are the envelopes, ready to carry the hot little cheques to all those kind suppliers who still give credit.

Here too is writer's block, a sudden, unexplained muscular resistance to gripping the pen combined with a mental reluctance to grapple with the figures. Between the words 'Pay' and 'or order' lies an empty, welcoming line, a tempting virgin space beside that big '£' sign waits expectantly for the pen, the bottom right-hand corner longs for a sweeping, confident autograph. What happens?

Scargill stubborn, the mind wanders. What does it mean, 'or order'? Are those strange computer blobs on the bottom the graphic equivalents of the bleeps and tweets that chirrup from space invaders machines? How is it that by writing out one of these slips of paper, I actually make myself poorer? Why does the map of Scotland on the Bank of Scotland cheques include Cumberland, Northumberland and Durham?

Funny things, invoices. Some firms need foot-square sheets of paper listing everything from the accountant's birthday to his girl friend's taste in Christmas presents to remind you of your £10 debt, while others dun you for £1,000 on little more than a slip of lined lavatory paper.

The ritual struggle to identify and subtract the hidden credit charges does something to stimulate the mind. Some want it paid after three weeks, some after three months. This one is at five per cent, that at ten. Here it is built into the unit price and you have to deduct it yourself; there it is slipped in high above the bottom line and you have all the fun of finding it.

On top of the festering heap of bills is one from a firm in the forefront of invoice technology, the cutting edge of business stationery. Once, opening their invoice was like receiving a personal letter. All the details were written out in immaculate script by a sweet-tempered lady who never made a mistake but was always on the end of the telephone if you had a query.

Where she would have put 'One vee belt . . . £7 10s 4d' the computer puts '09/02/85 Ref: ZX1879 Code 43–7776–19 Quantity one unit indi details ve bit rate vat code amount total cr dr ch br fwrd crdts' – and then, triumphantly printed right through all the multi-coloured copies 'TOTAL AMOUNT DUE £17.50.'

Even the simplest of these demands provides plenty of intriguing reading. Why do you suppose the Inland Revenue feels so strongly about cheques sent to them being *unfolded* (their italics)? How could 'cash received after the date of this statement' be 'shown above'? Why must shortages or errors be notified within seven days? Why does everybody remind their customers that 'Title to goods does not pass until payment has been received in full'?

All these pieces of paper are grains of sand drifting against the base of the great economic pyramid on top of which sit Nigel Lawson and the world's bankers. Among the grains is the bank statement, with the interest sucked out of it as painlessly as possible by the bank – no need to write out a cheque for that.

The best thing that could happen to me would be for the pound to drop below the dollar, thereby increasing the value of my wheat; and for interest rates to drop. So what does Nigel do? Ups interest rates in order to prevent the pound sliding.

Could we not just put this whole thing off for a couple of weeks and call our cramp-induced procrastination cash-flow management? The EEC considers it quite legitimate to save itself money by making us wait for ours.

That is the answer. It must be good economics to get in that cheque for the heifers, before writing out any more. Strange how different a cheque looks when it has your name top centre as opposed to bottom right. I've never yet got writer's block when confronted by a paying-in slip.

Not Known at this Address

Mr C. Shanley has moved into my home and is making a bid to run the farm. I have never seen the man, but he must be here because letters arrive for him almost every day.

I have taken to intercepting them, opening them, occasionally reading them and consistently throwing them away. It is unprincipled, I know – quite possibly it is criminal – but since he is apparently trying to ease me out of a job and has caused me one major matrimonial hiccup, I am not worried about principles or criminality.

At first his correspondence all had an agricultural flavour.

'Dear Mr Shanley, how would you like to actively improve

your bottom line profits?' inquired a combine manufacturer. 'Dear Mr Shanley, why aren't you using an in-feed growth promoter?' impertinently asked a major chemical company.

Of course Mr Shanley is the figment of some computer's vivid imagination. He has eased himself on to a mailing list which has been bought by several companies and he will probably live for ever.

But why would a famous scent manufacturer buy this agricultural list and land me in trouble?

'Dear Mr Shanley,' read the last missive I opened. 'Are you aware of the fragrance of today which envelops a woman in pure magic? Discover its magic. Pull this flap and . . .'

I pulled the flap and, sure enough, was enveloped in a scent which is, apparently, 'assertive, sensual, young and modern'. It is certainly better than silage or ammonia-treated straw; and it was certainly assertive enough to make my wife wonder with whom I had spent the morning. I mumbled about Mr Shanley and his scent-drenched letters, but . . .

I started planning ways to rid myself of the man. Returning his correspondence to the senders, unstamped and wrapped round bricks, seemed worth a try, but new bricks are expensive and every ounce of brick rubble round here is hoarded and saved for gateway maintenance.

A friend advised writing to the chairman of the companies concerned, pointing out that they were wasting pounds on postage – for there must be thousands of C. Shanleys around the country – but chairmen tend to be faceless, addressless men.

It was going to be difficult to bump the fellow off and were I to succeed in getting him eliminated from the lists, might his disappearance come to the attention of the authorities? Might I end up helping the police with their enquiries?

Mr Shanley, I shall have to let you live and make the best of having you around. I shall let you take over. How wonderful it will be when all the mail is addressed to you – except the cheques of course, but they are few and far between. You can fill in the June census and the FHDS forms and run the risk of prosecution if you are late with the VAT and tell the MAFF man in Guildford all he wants to know every month about cereals fed to cattle and wade through the bills and the invitations to subscribe to pension plans, book clubs, limited edition special offer figurines, and chances to win everything from a television voucher to a trans-Atlantic ticket for two on Concorde.

Dear Mr Shanley, you are just what we all need. 'Hello,' says the rep. 'Is the boss in?'

'No,' you can smile sweetly. 'Mr Shanley is not around at the moment. Telephone if you like. His number's in the book.'

Why should he remain a mister? 'I've got this load of hoggin, see, on the back of the lorry.' 'I'll tell Lord Shanley when he comes home, but being a circuit judge he is seldom here . . .'

Should work a treat.

My one piece of advice to you, nice Lord Shanley, dear Lord Shanley, is this: keep away from the sensual fragrance.

Animals Bring Out The Human In You

WE MEET SOME QUADRUPED FRIENDS; LEARN TO
TREAT ONE OF THEM WITH RESPECT; AND
ENCOUNTER THE PUNK

Anthropomorphism – That's My Trouble!

If you think Walt Disney's anthropomorphic approach to animals is nauseatingly sentimental, cloyingly cute and irredeemably yucky, then read no further. This will only make you feel ill.

But if you have ever thought of your stock in even faintly human terms, you can safely read on.

I have a bunch of about fifty in-calf cows and heifers, wintering outside, poaching the life out of a field that will be drilled with spring barley. The looks on their faces when they are fed on a shivering, sleety morning – with no prospect of sun, and the silage steaming in the mud, and snow at their feet – are, I think, distressingly recriminatory.

It is my fault they are outside, it is my fault the field is muddy, it is my fault the weather is foul; and their lowered heads, hunched flanks and reproachful eyes make it quite clear what they think of me for inflicting this treatment on them.

They slink out from the wood where they shelter at night,

pick disconsolately at their feed, and hurry back to the compara-
tive warmth of the trees. They are like a gang of resentful
prisoners, sullen and rebellious.

On a bright, hard, frosty morning, their demeanour changes
to that of a bunch of unruly children. They run about and bunt
each other on the hard ground, chasing and scrummaging
around the feed trailer, glad to be alive. They look grateful
instead of antagonistic, and one can leave them without feeling
guilty.

I do not think good stock farmers allow themselves to indulge
in this sort of rubbish. When they see the silage hit the mud
they are thinking of conversion ratios, digestible energy values,
MEs, NEs, and MJs per kg.

But ever since, as a child, I used to sit on the back of one
particularly friendly Ayrshire, I have never been able to prevent
myself attaching human characteristics to animals.

The Hereford bull, for instance, that is also wintering outside,
was born and bred in Scotland – and it shows. He is a great,
solid, dour, monosyllabic Scot. A Bill Shankly of an animal.

The Limousin heifer certainly knows she is the only pure-bred
female I have on the place. She is positively Parisienne in her
arrogance – and her bitchiness – bullying her smaller companions, remaining elegant on even the dirtiest morning. She is as
French as the bull is Scottish.

I once visited a farm where there were Gelbviehs, Chianinas,
Simmentals and several other exotic breeds, and the owner
swore they stuck together by nationality. I argued that animals
bred and brought up together always stuck together in a herd,
but he was convinced that they divided according to country of
origin.

In the field next to the outside beasts are the pregnant ewes,
showing all the human signs of pre-natal fulfilment. No matter
how cold the weather they graze away industriously – 'eating
for three, you know'.

Also eating furiously are the Billy Bunters of the farm, the
small group of bulls being intensively fattened on barley. Their
diet and weight makes them reluctant to stir from their bed of
clean straw; even when the food is brought in, they move only
slowly towards the troughs, like gross schoolboys, lumbering off
towards the tuck shop for another afternoon's guzzle.

Not only the farm animals display human characteristics.
Foxes, which seem to be for ever on the increase, share many of
the qualities of Machiavelli and Attila the Hun; and cock

pheasants and the Prince Regent seem to me to have much in common.

It is all very personal, of course. I could never anthropomorphize the chickens, for instance, although people do. And I find the trout have very little personality, although I dare say the fanatic trout farmer could develop favourites.

It is a bad habit. Milk yields did not drop when people stopped having a name for every cow in the parlour, and it certainly does not do for a dairyman to have favourites. I must remember that bullocks are not really individual characters, just killing-out percentages with legs.

The impersonal approach must make for more efficient agriculture. As an example, we once had a Hereford cross heifer around the farm for more than two years, eating her head off, before she was heavy enough to grade.

She just never seemed to grow – we kept her because she was rather pretty. What an embarrassing admission.

The Lamb with the Cauliflower Ear

Newly turned-out lambs running races in the wintry sunshine attract crowds that any politician would be proud of. This year, ours went out for the first time on a beautiful Sunday (flaming February, said the *Daily Express*, overdoing it as usual) and the bridle path beside their field was thronged with half-term walkers oohing and aahing and laughing at their antics.

Well, perhaps 'thronged' is a bit *Daily Express*, but at times there were twenty or more men, women, children and dogs looking over and through the fence.

Even the most hard-hearted carnivore must see a week-old lamb as more than merely legs, shoulders, saddle, succulent kidneys and chops. Even the most financially desperate of farmers must look on it as more than a prospective cheque. And even the most blinkered politician must feel it is not just a piece in the endless chess game with France – not only legs, but potential gigots, too.

Star of this year's lambing circus, which now is over, is a victim of baby battering who was nearly killed by his mother. 'Brave Lamb Beats Bashing Horror', the *Express* would say.

He was so butted and shoved around by the ewe that blood vessels in both his ears burst, and they filled with blood and caused him such discomfort that he went right off his bottle. He had never got any milk from his b-minded mum in the first place.

Apparently burst blood vessels are what cause cauliflower ears in boxers and lock forwards, although it puts them off neither bottle nor draught.

So I took him to the vet's. He rode on the front seat of the Land Rover, looking at the traffic with quizzical interest and bleating loudly and continuously.

The vet, pushed for space, operated on him outside the back door, standing him on a dustbin and cutting open his grotesque ears to let the blood spurt out. It did – with a vengeance. The back yard looked more like a scene from *M.A.S.H.* than *All Creatures Great and Small*, and the lamb wriggled so much that the stitches did not go in very straight, leaving him with a lop-sided grin on his face and a fully restored appetite.

Two ladies sitting in the waiting room with a cat to be spayed asked me – as I walked to wash the blood from my arms – if the crying they had heard had been a baby. What can they have thought we were doing out there on the dustbin?

The lop-eared hero is now cock of the walk in the orphanage, the bale enclosure where the triplets and other waifs and strays live.

Last year we lambed at exactly the same time as this year, but twelve months ago the drive up to the farm every midnight was through drifting snow and over an icy track. This year the nights have been summer mild, occasionally wet, but generally clear and starlit.

The people who ooh and aah would rightly count us lucky – those of us who help with deliveries in the middle of the night, who kneel beside the old ewes when they are having trouble, who see a wet lamb's first shake of the head and hear the mother start to nibble at the afterbirth on its nose.

When you fail to save a newly started life, you feel rotten, not because it represents £25 you are never going to see, but because so much pain, effort and waiting has come to nothing.

According to my new printout calculator, my lambing percentage this year has been 171.27659. That is not the point.

I remember talking to an old Scottish shepherd when I was young, who said that after years and years of lambings, he would still crouch under a dyke in the cold early morning to watch an old 'yow' starting her final push.

'It always makes me think of Christmas,' he said. 'You know something good is happening. You know you are doing something right.'

That is the point.

Sometimes Life is Very Sweet

Wherever it was that inspired the lines about autumn being the season of mists and mellow fruitfulness, I don't suppose it was Carlisle cattle market in October.

Nevertheless, it was Carlisle in the middle of the month that set my heart beating as rhapsodically as any poet's, so charged did I become with the beauty and excitement of the place, the tension of the ring, the majesty of the lairage, the grandeur of the cattle in the pens.

I was there to sell Samson, my young bull; he is, I can now reveal, a Limousin.

(Until now I have been bound by a year-long vow not to mention the word 'Limousin'; the promise was induced by my powerful sense of cowardice – I was getting a definite feeling that a posse of Charolais skin-heads and Hereford-breeding Hell's Angels was going to break every bone in my body if I did not keep quiet for a time about the Limousin's merits.)

For six years Carlisle has been the site of a series of Limousin sales and Samson was one of about 100 bulls there this month for the first of the season.

I had a feeling it would be a good day from the moment I got out of bed. I drove down to Carlisle from the Scottish farm. It was one of the few days of bright sunshine this rain-filled October has grudgingly allowed us and the Border countryside was at its dramatic best.

The dew on the fields was so heavy it looked like frost and the low early-morning sun made it sparkle on the grass while the light cast black shadows behind every tuft and hillock, heightening the greens and darkening the hollows, giving the leys the pattern of a camouflage jacket and striping newly ploughed stubbles with thick, exaggerated, bands.

Sheep in one place clustered round a Land-Rover for feed; in another they were lying motionless among equally immobile cattle; outside Annan they were being driven down the centre of the A75, causing consternation in the cabs of several Irish juggernauts heading for Stranraer.

Only the radio failed to catch the gentle mood of the morning, with Radio Scotland offering a report on 'The Lace-curtain Alcoholics of Suburbia' at 8.45 am, when a little Haydn would have been more appropriate.

I had handed the preparation of Samson over to a professional for this important occasion, for the sale was to be preceded by a show (judge, Mr Bud McBride from Alberta) and I did not think my amateur attempts at grooming and polishing would be up to Canadian standards.

Sure enough, he looked splendid (I mean Samson, not Bud – although Bud looked pretty good, too) and collected a third-prize rosette, which only goes to show how wise and perceptive they make them in Alberta – although not quite as wise and perceptive as in Anglesey, as we shall see.

I had never been to a major breed society sale before and did not know what a feeling of anticipation and excitement was in store. All auctions, of course, contain many of the elements of drama, but when you are selling an animal you have bred yourself, when the ring is packed to the ceiling, every steep tier full of faces, when it is all new to you, then the tension mounts as much as ever it does on a stage.

Samson sold well, and I went home happy. One minute I was worrying about reserves and how I would get him home again (oh me of little faith); the next, he was out of the ring and no longer mine – one of the best prices of the day paid for him by a wise and lovely man from, yes, Anglesey, obviously a natural and skilful judge of cattle.

On the drive home to Berkshire, Radio Three obliged with some Haydn, the sun continued to shine, even on Birmingham, children on their tatty holidays smiled as I passed, automatic harvesters picked the potatoes the childen were out of school to gather, and the alcoholics of suburbia stayed behind their lace curtains – out of sight, out of mind.

When I got home at dusk, the drill was just finishing a field of wheat, leaving us just seventy acres still to do; and to cap it all, the following day Southampton beat West Ham 3–0 at home. Sometimes life is very sweet.

My First and Last Foal

Births on this farm this year total about 300 lambs, thirty-five calves, four kittens, assorted ducklings, coot and moorhens, at least two hedgehogs, and dozens of other wild things I wot not of.

But the star of this 500-acre maternity ward and paediatric unit is the foal.

(Real farmers stop here. I know real farms do not have ponies, never mind foals, so if you can't stand things quiche, you had better move smartly on.)

I first saw him by torchlight at 3.00 am; he must have been about two hours old then and already he was up and sucking.

Isn't nature wonderful?

That's the kind of gushing comment that foals produce in people. Without exception every grown man who has seen it has oohed and aahed like the Mums over the prams outside Tesco (Well, Tesco seems to be the chief baby-admiration centre in our town; perhaps Sainsbury fills that role in yours.)

There was one exception to the oohs and aahs brigade. The local racing enthusiast watched it canter uncertainly across the paddock and said: 'Blimey, I've put money on slower things than that,' but then he sees everything as a potential good thing – even some of the cattle.

Did you ever have one of those children's books consisting of pictures of animals with each page split horizontally into three parts, so that you could create your own monster by matching up the head of a lion with the body of a zebra and the legs of a rhino?

The foal could well come out of that book with a mane borrowed from a punk hairstylist, tail out of a brush salesman's sample case, colouring weirdly like a Limousin and legs nicked from a giraffe.

But beauty is in the eye of the beholder and to me, he's lovely.

He's the first and last foal I shall ever be involved with; we bred from his mother for the worst of all possible reasons – because we wanted an excuse for keeping her after the children had grown out of her. 'What are you going to do with her foal?' asked one experienced breeder when I said we were looking for a stallion. 'I haven't thought,' I admitted. 'Huh, breeding dog-meat,' snorted the lady, quite justifiably.

Eleven months later the dog-meat was due. Having launched into the business thinking a foal's birth would be no different to a calf's or lamb's, my confidence ebbed and trepidation increased as the due date approached. 'You must sit up with her all night,' said some. 'Leave her out in the field,' said others. 'Keep her in the loose-box . . . just let her get on with it . . . visit her every few hours . . .' Advice came as freely as political promises.

In the end I settled on a last-thing-at-night, 3.00 am and first-thing-in-the-morning routine. She kept us in suspense for three weeks; milked like a Friesian for two; almost every evening I thought, 'This will be it; she looks really broody tonight.' Each morning, still no dog-meat.

Early, early in the morning after he was born, I went down to open the loose-box door and let proud mother and gawky son out into the paddock. It had rained hard in the night but the sun cut through the bright mist, dancing on the dew and bursting buds, setting them incandescing like summer sea-spray.

With all the innocence of his five hours on earth, he tottered into the great world, innocent of his future and ignorant of his surroundings, relying for confidence on his mother's warm flank.

Sorry. Gushing again. Truth insists that the sun also slanted on to the massive clumps of nettles I had not sprayed and the unrepaired wall of the field shelter; and as for the foal's future, he seems doomed to never-ending Pony Club camps and gymkhanas.

Meanwhile, every passer-by brings me a fresh report. 'He's been sleeping; he's cantering; he's trying to eat grass already.' I listen to it all with exactly the ill-justified pride that grand-mothers have in their grandchildren.

o6 and The Punk

This is the story of o6 and The Punk. OSix is an elderly
Hereford cross cow, unexceptional in every respect, and
The Punk is the pony foal who got his name from the way his
spiky black mane contrasts freakishly with his strawberry roan
coat.

The foal does his best to live up to his name. He can head-
butt a post-and-rail fence until the rails drop off; he puts the
boot in, quick as a flash, if you approach him when his head is
in a bowl of coarse mix; he needs a regular fix of leather which
he gets by chewing his companion pony's tack whenever possible; he broke out one night in winter and was brought back by
the police; and all this before his first birthday.

He lives in the field beside the lake. On the far side of the lake
is a belt of trees, then the river, then the water meadows in
which the cows, last week, were getting an early bite.

About half of them had calved, but not o6. I cannot imagine
it myself, but presumably it is confusing when you are feeling
maternal and have had several calves in the past, to see small
calves all around you, yet not have one to call your own.

In any event, o6 saw The Punk through the trees and across
the water and either decided to adopt him or, perhaps, thought
he was hers. She waded the river, swam the lake and went to
claim him.

He is a sort of Hereford colour, so the mistake was forgiveable,
but it was not going to be forgiven by The Punk. He nipped her,
chased her, kicked out and generally did a fair imitation of a
Chelsea supporter who has just glimpsed a Crystal Palace fan in
the Fulham Road.

Shocked by her reception, o6 swam back across the lake but
could not climb the bank on the far side. It was time to take a
hand. Number one son was sent for a halter and rope, number
two son fetched the boat and I sat on the bank pleading with
the old girl not to go into a stress-induced hypomag fit, which
seemed extremely likely, nor to experiment with that gynaecological technique which was in the papers recently and involves
giving birth underwater.

She looked exhausted, but before boat or halter could arrive
she summoned up her strength and put in another fifty metres
freestyle, back to the pony's shore. Before The Punk could

engage with her again I ran round, caught him, and tied him to the fence. All that remained now was to drive her out of the field, over the bridges and back to the meadows.

Relieved that the end of the drama was in sight I went to round her up, but she must have associated me with The Punk's Libyan behaviour because she lowered her head and had a go. Only a bash on the nose would persuade her to turn towards the gate.

She slowed to a walk. 'Look out,' I shouted to number one son who was at the exit from the field. 'She's quite distressed; she might have you.'

But once out of The Punk's territory, she regained her composure. For an hour or two she went round and round the meadows, inspecting all the other calves and dismissing them; she did not swim the lake again, nor did she get staggers.

In the afternoon, she calved without trouble. How we cure The Punk of his negative attitude towards cows, and turn him into a fulfilled and contributing member of society, I am not quite sure.

I Didn't Get a Kick Out of This

We were halfway through the routine business of sorting out the calves for worming when the sun dropped from the sky, Everest toppled and Berkshire shifted violently on its axis.

I have been kicked often enough by cows and calves to treat their back legs with respect.

It is second nature not to get too close and always to be ready to take evasive action, but on this particular morning I was caught by a couple of glancing kicks on the knee, which I attributed to old age and slowing reflexes.

They were just cuffs, nothing when compared with the afternoon attack.

I think the culprit was a little bull about six months old, but I could not recognize him because everything went so blindingly black, purple and red that I could not see the mugger in question.

He lashed out with both feet simultaneously like a bucking horse and, as accurately as Marciano landing a right on an opponent's chin, he smashed his two hooves into the most tender part of my anatomy.

Only if it has happened to you will you understand the

sickening pain. It is much worse than any broken leg or nose that I have ever suffered, and two days later it is still with me. For years I have been picking the bulls which I think will put extra muscle into their calves' back ends but I never intended the muscle to be used in anger against me.

'Is there anything you can do, doctor?' I asked. 'Not much,' he said, trying not to smile, and he handed out some pain killers which seem to make me ache and shiver so much that the cure is worse than the ailment.

Collapsed in front of the television for a Two Ronnies repeat, it suddenly strikes me how many of their jokes are about people getting kicked or hit in the privates. 'A bit touchy about the credentials, are you?' asks one of the Ronnies and everybody falls about laughing. I no longer see the joke.

The only comedian's catch phrase which suddenly has taken on a new meaning is: 'It only hurts when I laugh, doctor.' Or cough. Or clear my throat. Or stand. Or sit. Or walk. Or lie. Or eat. Or drink . . . and the painkillers' bottle states baldly: 'AVOID ALCOHOL'.

So there is the lesson for this week. However experienced and careful you are with cattle, don't relax your guard.

Trading The Tools Of The Trade

Wellies to Boot

Let us now consider the most important equipment on any farm: the wellies.

Slumped inside the door, waiting like loyal dogs to be taken walking by their owner, muddied wellies are as much symbols of the British winter as Damart catalogues and bulletins on Bryan Robson's ligaments.

Like the poor, wellies are always with us, our companions through the quagmires, our protection against insidious slurry.

I am too young to remember life before the welly. Did the state of feet and condition of the anaerobic areas between the toes depend on stout leather and dubbin . . . dubbin as applied to the solid, rounded toes of my first football boots . . . dubbin, with a feel, smell and taste which still live in my dark memories of the school boot-room?

My ancient encyclopaedia has pages on costume, but scarcely a mention of boots except a suggestion that they were a sign of status in ancient Greece. There is a picture of Assyrian warriors who appear to be going to war in their wellies, but the illustration of the fourteenth-century ploughman shows him walking the fields in little more than a pair of long johns while his yuppie contemporaries favoured shoes pointed enough to make 1960s winkle-pickers look stunted in comparison.

Unlike the Greeks, I find it hard to see any sort of boot as a status symbol. Of course, I am aware of the enormous significance of the green wellie, but overriding its social implications and role as a personal statement is a far bigger conundrum. Why does it have a buckle? No matter how you adjust it, it does not make the thing any more waterproof or less uncomfortable.

I confess to once having owned a pair of green wellies, and many a morning I have spent crawling around the yard in the half light, retrieving used Kleenex and cat-rejected fish heads because the redundant buckle has sliced open the bulging rubbish bag and interrupted my pre-breakfast routine by freeing half the contents.

Wellies are lovely when they are new, genuinely dry within and slapping crisply against shin and calf as you walk. But as the months pass they become perceptibly less waterproof and softer. Do not pretend that you walk the winter fields wondering what to give the wife for Christmas, if set-aside is a viable policy or whether the decimal point is in the right place in your margin-over-concentrates figure.

No. You are the same as everyone else. The great conundrum with which you wrestle is this: IS THIS DAMPNESS IN THE SOCKS CAUSED BY MOISTURE COMING OUT FROM THE FOOT OR IN THROUGH THE BOOT?

My encyclopaedia gives no clue as to how the wellie acquired its name, and pages of biography of the first Duke of Wellington give no hint of whether the eponymous boot was born outside Poona or Madrid, or whether, in fact, the great commander-in-chief had anything to do with its birth.

I have my own theory. Lurking in the unexpected clamminess of the wellie's dank interior is the miasma of an infection which invades the sock, seeps into the sole of the foot and marches up through the body before camping in the sinuses, behind the eyes and between the ears. Beechams powders, Vitamin C, hot whisky and all the skills of the homeopath are powerless before its great forced march to victory.

The common cold is as relentless, well organized and disciplined as a great military leader, which explains the name given to its source and origin: the Wellington boot.

Wellie Purchase Feasibility Study

A major management and investment decision is about to be taken on this farm, and I do not mind admitting that I have spent the last seven days wrestling inconclusively with the problem.

Under analysis is the business of the leaking right wellie. Will it see me through the winter or should a new pair be bought?

This is the kind of short-term capital investment appraisal, with twelve-month depreciation and nil terminal value, which lends itself readily to a discounted cash-flow analysis (or DCF as we familiarly call it over a pint in the bar of the Happy Heifer.)

'Can't seem to get the same figures from the DCF as the linear programme,' is the sort of thing you often hear Old Eli mutter into his bitter, and the wellie purchase feasibility studies have made me know how he feels.

I started off trying for a straightforward estimate of 'rate of return'. That did not get very far, because in trying to assess what the profit on the investment was likely to be I was led immediately into a desperate, struggling attempt to define 'profit'.

Dry feet, less unpleasant socks, less disincentive to walk through the bogs we call cattle yards . . . these were all obvious elements of profit, but where do they fit into the cashflow?

Then there was the problem of what figure to put in for 'capital required'. Should I put down the purchase price of both boots? Or just do an opening valuation on the right one, since the left will not be used until its predecessor springs a leak to match that in the right?

It does seem to be distorting the figures unacceptably to put in exactly double the actual immediate cash requirement, although my judgement is that it will not be long before the left one will attain obsolescence.

This factor also greatly complicates the estimate of economic life and rate of depreciation calculations. So you will readily appreciate that I had to go for the more sophisticated DCF method of appraisal, taking into account the internal rate of return, discounted yield, time value of money and variability of the cash-flow rate.

By discounting the negative cash flow one year back and using the usual formula for annuities $(1 - 1/(1+r)^n \div r)$ I came up with a net deficit on the investment so frighteningly large that I would not dare take my figures to the bank manager.

What to do?

Obviously it was necessary to take a view on the likely consequences of retaining the *status quo* and not making the investment. But how to quantify the effect of a winter of soggy socks? After all, slight sogginess can be lived with . . . and BUPA should cover any major attendant complications.

However, never let it be said that my investment parameters are circumscribed by the need to attach figures to everything . . . if that were so I would never have built into the purchase decision assessment module my forecast of possible future changes in wellie demand, supply, price, cost and technology.

That last is most important; how the accountant would laugh at me if I were to take the plunge into new wellies now, when, unknown to me, a whole new breakthrough in wellie technology was on the horizon, making redundant (and, what's worse, valueless) the wellie we know and love today.

Nervous, uncertain, indecisive, stripped of all confidence, I turned for help in my decision to a combination of matrix construction and cumulative capital balance accounting which obviates the uncertainty of the more deterministic models and properly evaluates resource levels and requirements together with net revenue ratios.

I have now combined that with the whole farm budget appraisal, and I think I am very close to taking the definitive wellie decision. What I might just do first, however, is wander into town and see what the things cost.

Dress Sense

Few of life's glittering prizes lie within our reach. The Nobel Committee and the Academy of Motion Picture Arts and Sciences consistently ignore farmers in their nominations, as do *Radio Times* readers when voting for the Sports Personality of the Year.

Deprived of the hope of a Peace Prize, Oscar or silver-plated

model of a television camera, we are left to dream of a ploughing
trophy or our names on the local bar billiards shield.

But now a local Berkshire menswear firm has come up with a
competition in which farmers ought to sweep the board year in,
year out: the search is on for Britain's scruffiest man, and if that
is not a title that should be perpetually linked with agriculture,
then my name is Boy George.

It was a glimpse of myself in the mirror during the cold
weather, and the sight of several snow-bound friends coming in
from work, which made me realize we could walk this one.

You must have noticed how the clothes sold as country-wear
in this country are shamefully inadequate. How often during the
last month have you wondered why modern science has yet to
solve the problem of keeping heat in and wet out? Were you
disheartened by the news that years of research have failed to
produce an army boot which does not rot the average para's
toes after a couple of days' yomping?

After many winters of suffering, I am on my way to beating
the problem with a series of garments which have only one thing
in common: none of them is designed for ordinary outdoor,
agricultural wear. Neat quilted waistcoats and smart green
jackets leave me cold. In the bleakest mid-winter, I am to be
found inside a parka from a mountaineering shop, a jacket
designed for off-shore sailing, a skier's socks and polo-necked
jerseys and thermals designed by a famous pair of dinghy racers.

Hence my interest in the scruffiest man competition.

Not only is the overall effect distinctly – as Yves St Laurent
never said – *'déco-ordonné'* – but the *ensemble* is also torn, worn,
stained and, to be brutally frank, definitely fragrant with a
distinctive sheepy, silagey, dieselly scent which is not to be
found in the Yves St Laurent range either.

Most farmers are similarly scruffy, yet who walked away with
last year's Britain's Scruffiest Man title? A London student and
wine-bar worker called John Hamilton.

'Was he as scruffy as the average farmer?' I asked one of the
competition organizers. 'Well,' she said. 'He was unbelievably
scruffy. His photograph was really amazing.'

She was so easily impressed, I do not think she can ever have
seen a farmer. I can only think of a single reason why one should
not claim the title this year: the prize. No true scruff would want
to win it.

The champion will have £1,500-worth of jackets, trousers and
shirts pressed upon him, his wardrobe filled with flash new
suitings, his wreck of a body re-upholstered from his ten-inch

trouser bottoms, through his inside-leg measurement to his discreet shoulder pads. Then he will be presented with . . . The Changed Man Award.

Personally, I would not want a Changed Man Award even if they got Felicity Kendal or Joanna Lumley to make the presentation. Well, perhaps Joanna Lumley.

Aware of the natural modesty of the male, the competition organizers have deviously arranged for the entries to be made by wives, girlfriends, grannies or daughters. All they have to do is send a photograph of the unhappy contender, plus a description of him in less than 100 words.

Women are born with the reforming zeal of Calvin which they never lose; they cannot completely accept that they will never convert their old man into Slurryhurst's answer to Omar Sharif or Terry Wogan. To be Britain's scruffiest man may be well within his reach; but the Changed Man Award seems a glittering prize with flaking plating.

Hands Up All You Bargain Hunters

'Lot 112: four vices,' called the auctioneer from within the jostling crowd of broad backs.

'I've got two of them already: gluttony and sloth,' said my companion, the rain running from the tip of his nose. 'There will be hell to pay if I take home four more.'

Through the mud, we shuffled on to the next lot, 'quantity tools', as invisible as the auctioneer. How do people know the value of these odds and ends? Saleroom freaks will tell you that the beauty of an auction is that the value of everything is firmly established – it is what someone will pay for it there and then.

That may be so in the suave surroundings of Christie's and Sotheby's, where pinstriped ex-Guards officers quietly catch bids which electronic display boards simultaneously convert into Yen, Deutschmarks, Dollars and Swiss Francs; but Bond Street and St James's Street are a million miles from this sodden field and the Duke of Devonshire's drawings have nothing in common with lot 115, 'quantity sharpening stones'.

A well-attended farm sale can see things sold for far more than they are worth. That afternoon in the rain, old wheelbarrows fetched more than those on offer in the local builders' merchants and once in the past I found myself offering way over the odds for some second-hand disc harrows simply because I had not done my homework and did not know what they cost new.

The excitement of the auction is infectious – except when you are among the sellers. To whomever bought my auger for £18 at the racecourse sale last year – you got a bargain.

If only I knew for sure the worth of these things, I would be bidding with the rest of them, but my Scots blood makes me fear the thought that I might go over the top. 'Mangle and pump'. 'Sheet of brass'. 'Wire ropes'. I would love to bear them home in triumph, confident I had made a smart deal, but the opportunities march past like soldiers in quick time and I never raise my hand in salute.

What I am after is not Lot 139 'towing chain', although you can never have enough towing chains, nor 'quantity forty-gallon drums' nor 'wooden staircase'. I want a bigger fish – a good second-hand combine. When we get to it, all confidence ebbs. What do I know about second-hand combines? Would you buy a used combine from this man? Suddenly the great machine looks like a pig and the sale is definitely a poke.

If no one bids, then obviously there is something wrong with it. If everyone is interested, then it will be too expensive . . . there is the insoluble dilemma of the inexpert farm sale customer.

On, on, the tide shifts onwards and the chance is lost. Who could possibly want all that used barbed wire? The lesson to be learned here is that nothing should ever be thrown away, for when you reach the last stop before the bailiffs – your own farm sale – everything will go, if only to the scrap man.

Old buckets, cracked slates, broken bricks – all will find an owner.

How embarrassing it will be though, to have the neighbours round inspecting the forgotten rubbish hauled from the dustiest nook and darkest cranny of your barn and workshop.

As when a burglar has rifled through your shirts and under-wear, you will be stripped of your pretences and stand naked for all to see – the man who over-ordered the Rumevite by twenty-five tonnes, who never threw away the milk churns, who collected more bent staples than straight ones.

'Lot 202: a chain vice.'

'That's a new one, I can't resist that,' said my companion, generously starting the ball rolling at fifty pence.

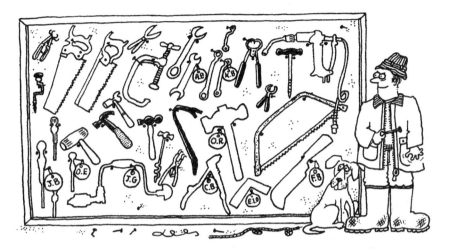

Tools of the Trade

One day we shall have a board in the barn on which all the tools will be painted in outline. There will be little discs with each man's initials written on them. When somebody takes a tool, he will hang his disc in the space so a glance at the board will reveal who has the large screw-driver, small wrench and claw hammer.

One day. One day we shall not need tools because machines will not break; and flying pigs need no servicing.

Meanwhile, the question 'who's got the tools?' remains unanswered and not because of the absence of a silhouette-covered board. The massive tool box, which is the farm's portable workshop, was left in the combine cab for a couple of rainy days. When we returned for it, it had gone for a walk accompanied by the shiny new fire extinguisher.

Tools enjoy a walk. That is why they are sold to you pinned by clear plastic to sheets of bright cardboard. If the shops did not shackle the screw-drivers to the shelves in this way, they would walk straight out of the door without pausing at the till. It is called shrinkage in the retail trade.

As soon as you get the things back to the farm and release them from their restraints, nine times out of ten they celebrate freedom with a quick walk-about, but a mass march of our entire collection of tools is a first on this farm.

In the stolen box was that funny pair of pliers with the bend in them that lets you reach the catches for the stone trap on the combine. There was the whatsit thing which gets at nuts round corners. And Fred Trueman, the hammer with the big back end.

Old allies, all gone. I do not know where half of them came from, for while tools walk off the farm, it is only fair to admit that frequently they walk on as well. If a fitter leaves a particularly attractive adjustable on the barn floor when he leaves, it seems gentlemanly to look after it for him for a few years in case he should ever come looking for it.

Off to buy replacements then, chequebook in hand. Since Draper Tools sponsors Southampton Football Club, I would like to buy Draper, thereby helping to finance the purchase of a new defender to replace Kevin Bond. You can get a good used full back for £50,000 if you know the right people.

But Draper was nowhere to be found in the temple of tools in which I eventually offered up my money. I am not a tool worshipper, or, in the children's current slang, a tool-head. I do see a kind of attraction in all those ranks of gleaming spanners and matt black screw-drivers, but I have always greatly admired the real tool-heads who can take one look at a nut and know without hesitation that an open-ended twenty-three metric will fit it.

When I try visually to size up a nut, I am faced with one decision: do I take twenty spanners out of the barn and try them all? Or do I make twenty trips to the barn and try one spanner at a time?

The priest officiating behind the counter in the temple sold me £129.99 worth of heavy metal. As I browsed through his shelves, I felt a strange sort of addiction coming over me. I was mysteriously attracted to implements and devices, the likes of which I had never seen before; and I learnt the names of old friends – I always believed, for example, that adjustable pliers were technically known as thingamebobsyouknows (as in 'hand me those thingamebobs, you know, yep them') but now I have learned that they are really called water pump pliers. I wonder why.

For a time I toyed with trying the minimalizing approach to tools. Could we operate on two big adjustables, a heavy hammer, plenty of wire, baler twine – and NOTHING ELSE?

The prospect seemed attractive, but just as the Moonies grip some, the Toolies got to me and I exchanged money for a couple of sets of long, strong, attractive spanners, one metric and one A/F. When I get the chance I shall silhouette them all on a board in the barn and . . .

In Praise of Part Players

L ast week the theft of the tool box gave rise to some thoughts
 on those fortunate people who enjoy and understand tools –
spanner-heads.

This week, problems in obtaining a part for the big baler have
reminded me that their enthusiasm is just part of a far greater
mystery, the complex world of parts and stores.

Thank goodness the farming world contains miracle-working
store-men who can pick the smallest sprocket or flange from
deep within their mysterious library of shelves without a
moment's hesitation. To those of us who suffer from a kind of
mechanical dyslexia, their skill is a wonder as great as a
composer's or playwright's. They arrange and recall bits and
pieces with all the genius that Mozart applied to notes or Ibsen
to words.

Get a true parts-head on the other side of the counter and
your problems are over. They understand and translate, like the
friendliest kind of analyst, thus:

'Er, I need one of those bits which holds up the plunger
outside the bracket on the baler.'

'That's a C478/991. They're up here. There you go. Anything
else?'

Parts-heads are born, not made. Get the wrong man, and it's
a very different story:

'What year is your baler?'

'Eighty-four or '85 I think.'

'Which?'

'I can't remember.'

'What's the serial number?'

'I've no idea.'

'Show me the part on this exploded picture then.'

'That does not seem to me to be a picture of my baler at all.
Why are all these cogs and wheels hovering above it? Why are
the shafts floating away in front?'

Once you have established which bit you need, the real fun
begins. Enter the boy who is in the parts department for three
weeks as part of the Youth Opportunity Programme. This
sallow, callow, part-time amateur football hooligan is known by
all and sundry as YOP, a strangely appropriate sound, and

much time and effort is devoted to thinking up things for him to do.

'YOP! Fetch a C478/991. They're round the back, up the top, near the gaskets. You'll need the steps.'

Off shuffles YOP, already looking mystified by the whole affair, as if the vast array of indispensable odds and ends was some kind of surrealist, decorative labyrinth, never intended to serve any useful purpose.

YOP returns. 'No. That's not a C478/991. The part numbers are in the cards on the bottom of the bins. Here, I'll show you. Again.'

Mind you, my sympathies are with poor confused YOP. As I say, parts-heads are begotten, not created.

The particular baler part I needed was not to be found, in any bin, on any shelf, either locally or nationally. I had an international parts problem, a sort of one-upmanship in which I do not want to indulge because you do not know where it will end. In this case the trail led to a store outside Brussels, but I noticed 'Made in Japan' stamped on an adjacent bearing and I have no wish to get involved with the Tokyo spares futures market.

The Belgian service worked surprisingly well. Reports of my bit came in from Felixtowe or Folkestone or somewhere (I was shockingly uninterested in the details), and it moved rapidly until caught in the quicksand of British Rail. I feared the worst but it popped up at the local station, proving that Europarts-heads thrive. (In Germany, are they dedicated to locating the parts that Mein Herr cannot reach?)

Where would we be without these enthusiasts?

And Now The Weather . . .

ISOBARS AND LOW PRESSURE DEMONSTRATE
THAT LIFE IN ARCADY IS TRULY GOVERNED BY
MIGHTY COSMIC FORCES

The Kettley Factor Takes Control

We have worked out a method of interpreting the strange jumble of facts and figures which BBC television calls the weather forecast. It is not an infallible system but it is better than nothing.

A team of three is needed, each with precisely defined responsibilities. One watches John Kettley's lips and tries to understand what he is saying, rather in the manner of the lip-reading experts hired by some newspapers to decipher the Duchess of York's every fleeting remark on her wedding day; another concentrates on the top left-hand corner of the screen where the vital words appear – today, tomorrow, tonight and so on; the third analyst concentrates on our particular patch of England to see whether little rays of sunshine, snowflakes or rain-filled clouds are superimposed on Berkshire.

Ideally, each viewer has a stopwatch so that during the post-forecast debriefing session we can synchronize all the information we have gleaned. Otherwise the conversation during the transmission runs rather like this:

'Tomorrow! It's tomorrow now.'
'But he's talking temperatures.'
'No, there's sunshine coming out of the bottom of the clouds over Dorking.'
'That's not sunshine, those are isobars.'
'Don't be stupid, he finished with the isobars ages ago.'
'WAKE UP DAD.'
'UUGH?'
'Who cares about Dorking?'
'It's still tomorrow – no, it's not, it's gone back to tonight.'
'Then it's raining.'
'It's not. Look out of the window.'
'NO. DO NOT LOOK OUT OF THE WINDOW. You'll miss the summary.
'Oh. No summary tonight. Turn it off.'

As I say, this is not an infallible system. For example, we have a particular local difficulty: it requires a sharp enquiring brain and quick eye to differentiate between the Isle of Wight and a raindrop falling out of a cloud over Basingstoke. But all in all it works quite well when the whole team is fit, trained and working together like a well-oiled machine.

British Telecom's weather forecast is more local, more accurate and can be understood single-handed. I'm surprised it is not sponsored like the speaking clock, but possibly it is difficult to find sponsors for bad news.

This preoccupation with the weather is even more obsessive than usual because of the nightmarish memories of my last year's harvest which, it is revealed by the final figures for sales which I have just received, resulted in 371 tonnes of marketable wheat from 203 acres drilled.

I am glad I do not know how much was beaten into the ground by the rain (£10,000 worth?) but the spectre of all that waste haunted and ruined even one beautiful evening a few weeks ago when we were in the thick of combining the winter barley with everything running smoothly. It should have been undiluted pleasure but fretting about the changeable weather spoiled it. Surely this year cannot be a repeat of last?

Now, in the middle of August, the barley is finished and we are still waiting for the wheat to ripen. It is several years since last we had such a gap between the barley and wheat and I had forgotten how frustrating it is to have fine weather and nothing fit to cut . . . especially at this time of year.

I have always been taught that 'when you think the corn is ready for the combine, wait a week'. That is going to be a difficult maxim to follow this year.

Scotch Wrath

Retribution comes with biblical swiftness to those who taunt the gods. If they are Scottish gods, the vengeance is particularly terrible.

No sooner had I dropped my last article into my friendly, local, privatized post-box, than threatening storm clouds began to gather on the horizon. Building, burgeoning, darkening, they rolled into the valley as if summoned by Cecil B. de Mille. A single streak of lightning cracked from their purple depths and rain deluged down as if someone had filled a king-size plastic bag with water, hoisted it into the sky, then run a Stanley knife along its swollen base from end to end.

And I thought I saw a face like Graeme Souness, and heard a voice like Bill Shankly, and the voice said: 'Don't whitter on, laddie, about the weather being kind to you Southerners. The harvest is yet to come, and I've hardly started on 'e'.

Too late, I realized my mistake. I had tempted the fates by writing about the kindness of the weather down here compared to the cold, wet misery the Scots are enduring; without hesitation, the fates rose and took the bait.

For the past week a grey drizzle has dripped from the grey clouds, drizzle of a kind I have only previously seen blowing in off the Atlantic to the Western Isles, yet here it is on the Southern Downs.

Thin, chill and pervasive, it seeps down the back of the neck and through the knees of trousers. Like the overdraft, it will not go away.

Did I boast last week that my winter barley was still standing? Slowly, undramatically, it is giving up and lying down a little more each day. It is as if the dreariness of the weather was making it hang its head, then slump its shoulders, before finally bringing it to its knees.

More theatrically, the wheat is going down as well, in great straight-edged horizontal circular patches where the wind catches it under overhanging trees. On the fringes of the flattened areas, the plants twist and tilt at improbable angles, awaiting the next storm and a chance to play the death scene. And a week ago they all looked so strong and healthy.

The wheat smells moist, the barley tastes mealy, the straw of both feels soft and cold. The rain soaks right inside the plants, permeating through them from top to root.

Dotted all over the surrounding countryside are combines, literally stopped in their tracks, marking by their brightly coloured presence the exact spot reached when the heavens opened. As I write, they have been silent for a week; motionless much longer, they will need planning permission.

Did I say last week that the river was running as clear as a chalk stream should? Not any more. Like a burn in spate, it is swollen and brown. Its mood has changed from a bright cheerfulness to a sullen, slow, moroseness.

Wherein lies redemption? What must we do to persuade the Souness/Shankly combination to relent and permit some sunshine on our combines? If all we Sassenachs do our bit for the Scottish economy and put away large quantities of the national product – the one that comes in bottles – can we buy ourselves some forgiveness?

Eyesores Revealed By Winter Gales

Like many women, and most men, the countryside looks more attractive clothed than stripped naked.

No, I am not bidding for the job of *Playboy's* agricultural correspondent. I am just bemoaning the heartless way the recent gales have torn the leaves from the trees almost before they have had a chance to turn; and there, revealed for another winter, are all the eyesores that summer foliage mercifully conceals.

First of these annual irritations is the reappearance of The Trespasser, who every weekend morning walks a private path that runs close to my house but, until the gales, was screened from view by alders.

Do not misunderstand. We have many trespassers. Some are lost, charming, glamorous (interested, Mr Hefner?), polite or apologetic. Others are insistent on their 'rights', abusive, threatening or stubborn. The Trespasser is all the latter, and persistent into the bargain.

I recently wrote him a long, polite letter, setting out the

reasons I would like him to stop walking on my land, but he appears regularly, conspicuous on the path beyond the now bare trees, flagrant in pale blue denims, his dog bounding in front.

In reply to my letter, he asked what harm he was doing. It seems inadequate to say that he is annoying me and certainly extravagant to apply for an injunction against him (which I believe I am entitled to do). Either I shall push him in the river one day, or take morning walks in his garden.

The denims are not the only flashes of colour revealed this autumn. That discarded mould-board plough (remember them?), thrown in a pit years ago, still shows brightly blue; strange, when the paintwork on new machines chips off so readily and is replaced so quickly by a camouflaging coating of rust.

Old fertilizer bags, too, blown to unexpected corners by the wind, emerge more vivid than ever from behind their concealing greenery.

Buildings reappear as well. Planners and architects have a standard ploy when they are putting something ugly where it should not be. Meticulously drawn on their plans are dozens of trees, planted as screening, intended to conceal their monstrosity from sight. Somewhere among the plans will be an architect's impression of the finished work and in the background will be a great wood of oaks and beeches. But have you ever seen an architect's drawing of the site in winter – all branches and trunks and gaps between?

Even the Forestry Commission seems sometimes to forget that leaves fall in November. Their new small woods scheme is not intended to give grants to coniferous plantations, yet only conifers can give a full year's concealment to an eyesore.

I hope it will make an exception to its rules when the wood is intended as a screen.

Also disclosed to every passing eye is the terrible state of the old woods themselves; it was good to read that the Countryside Commission is worried about the neglected state of small woods and copses – neglect caused entirely by unwelcome economies. Fallen limbs lie where they land; dead trees rot where they stand. I could keep a gang of woodmen employed throughout the winter with no trouble at all, could I only afford it. Oh, for the days of foresters and estate workers.

The gales have brought compensations, however. There is no need to sweep leaves from the lawn; they have all been blown off and piled in drifts, like snow, behind the nearest windbreak. The trick is to burn them where they lie, before the wind veers and blows them back on to the grass.

That is just one job on the list of projects for the winter – projects which stand a pretty slim chance of ever getting started. Get in a skip and load it with all rubbish; keep the power saw in perpetual use; burn leaves.

And The Trespasser? Well, what would *you* do about him?

What a Beautiful Morning!

A morning when Postman Pat brings only one bill is a good morning. It happened today. Things were unusually bright even before the struggle with the Post Office standard-issue rubber bands and the ritual progress through circulars, buff envelopes, exclusive American Express invitations, terribly important VAT notices and promises of great riches from *Reader's Digest*, in search of an unexpected grant cheque or subsidy payment.

In our house the curtains do not meet very well, so you can tell as soon as you have forced open an eye what sort of morning it is. That first impression of the weather dictates what kind of day lies in wait. When the low morning sun bounces off a hard frost like stage lighting, white and unnaturally dazzling, the next sixteen hours promise well. When there is no sun the curtains are framed in a funereal greyness that makes you think your sight is failing and you know you are doomed to a day of gloom.

But this morning was a stage-set morning, complete with mist dissolving and burnished beech trees. It looked like a one-bill morning and it was; and there were further proofs that the weather governs a great deal more than the state of the going at Wincanton.

On a stage-set morning you can get through the pre-breakfast chores without even knowing you are doing them. Shaving, riddling the Aga, taking out the rubbish should be as much mindless routine as pulling on trousers, best done with no conscious thought at all. But a broken zip or blunt blade, like an early call from a rep, can shatter the somnambulant rhythm of things and ruin the whole day. But reps ring, zips jam, only after the funereal awakenings.

All the dark fields, except two, now have neat green lines traced upon them. The wheat has germinated. On a stage-set morning, I think of it that way round, concentrating on the ninety per cent good news. On a funereal day, the two fields obviously stricken with the dreaded misty rot or frosty blight obscure the thousands of healthy plants.

The first job today was to try to establish why the straw oven is not improving D values and crude proteins as much as it should. This morning it seemed a simple, pleasant, straightforward task. In the rain it would have been a curse of a worry.

One possibility is that I have underestimated the weight of the bales. So I tied one on the back of the Land Rover and took it up to our nearest weighbridge which happens to be in the local scrapyard.

The sun lit up the rusting Renaults and stripped Cortinas as if they had been painted in oils. The scrap man, who took my beloved first car when I was twenty-one and broke her up for parts, and who would lose to Marvin Hagler in a charm contest, benignly took me to his 'museum' and cheerfully showed me round his ancient vehicles and collection of old coach lamps. Would he have done that if it had been raining?

Came home to a telephone call. Wheat destined for dog biscuits has been rejected. Go up to the grain store and find that one of the low-volume fans has seized up. In the crisp sunshine, what does it matter? You think you have problems? You could be Ronald Reagan's make-up man.

In the afternoon I took the gun and renewed the long-standing war against the Canada geese. I have been too tolerant with these pests but the sight of more than 300 of them treating my winter barley as if they had a right to it got my blood up. Winter barley is to Canadas as ganja is to Rastafarians, but there will be no no-go areas on this farm.

On gloomy days I have been made to look a complete idiot by the geese, chasing them from field to field gaining nothing but rust on the gun. This afternoon, in the sunshine, I shot eight, which does not reduce the numbers much but it makes them nervous and me feel better.

Furthermore, they died cleanly. Canadas are protected by an inch or more of feathers and often have a messy way of dying, flapping around wounded or running embarrassing distances. But today, execution was as clean as surgery. I am certain it would not have been if the sun had not been setting in a furious, red, frost-promising blaze.

Farewell to Old Friends

First light came reluctantly on the morning of Friday, 16 October 1987, embarrassed to reveal the gigantic vandalism wrought in the night, ashamed to show the evidence, the grey panorama of smashed fences, uprooted trees, abandoned branches.

The previous evening the barometer dropped faster and lower than I had ever seen it. As plainly as if it could speak, it told me that something exceptional was going to happen, but the television weather forecast predicted nothing out of the ordinary.

By two o'clock in the morning it was obvious that I was right and the television wrong. While the windows rattled and the whole house seemed to moan, I lay in bed, mentally patrolling the fences in the fields in which the sheep and cattle were grazing, noting in my mind's eye the areas threatened by particularly old or vulnerable trees.

I worked out how far the stock could stray, were they to wander through the gap in a smashed fence, and told myself it would be both pointless and dangerous to go out to check them in the dark.

Despite my anxieties, buildings and stock all survived and all the broken fences were by chance in empty fields. The trees were less fortunate. As with friends, so with trees: you only appreciate how much you liked them when they are gone.

There is only one tree on the place for which the family has a name, and thank goodness he survived. Doug the Douglas Fir is still standing just a few yards from the house, although one of his upper branches is stuck in the plough about fifty yards north of him.

(Doug got his name from football matches on the lawn. His bottom branches lie along the grass, giving him superb ball control. Slip him a through ball and he will hold it for hours while the strikers puff into position on the far post. Some say he's getting a bit slow, but at 150–200 years old, that's not surprising and there's no question of putting him on the transfer list. Now he has repaid our loyalty by staying upright through the hurricane. I thought the lad did super, Brian.)

Although anonymous, several of the dozen big fallen trees were friends almost as good as Doug. You feel comfortable with a familiar view, just as you feel comfortable in the company of an old acquaintance, but a view should be permanent. It is shocking to discover it can be torn apart like paper.

I was surprised to discover that people who have never mentioned views or beauty feel emotionally attached to my trees. 'Yes, you can replant,' said someone who has never before showed any trace of poetry in his soul, 'but something beautiful was destroyed last night as surely as if an old master had been slashed. The difference is that it is harder to restore. The scars from this attack will show for 100 years.'

Once the roads had been cleared, the problem was deciding which of the fallen to tackle first. We selected an enormous beech which was sticking, as incongruously as a seaside pier, into the field we had ploughed and readied for drilling. At the other end of the list of priorities is a lime in a grass park which I suspect will lie untouched for months.

In future, people will tell of gales and storms. I hope that when I am grey-bearded and terminally boring I shall be able to say with accuracy: 'Ah, but that is nothing compared with the morning of 16 October 1987.' I never want to see a dawn like that again.

Home and Garden Intrude

Macadamized Monologue

'*Morning, guv'nor. Lovely place you've got here. Lovely day. Look,
this is what I'm calling about. I run this tar-laying machine, see.
Well this winter it got completely snowed up, couldn't get near it for weeks
we couldn't, and when the thaw came, I thought we'd never be able to use
it again. Anyway, it's taken all this time to get it cleaned out. Had to get
it done because we start this big motorway contract tomorrow.*

'*Now they say they won't let me start on the motorway until we've given
the machine a trial, so what I'm looking for is a stretch of drive to
resurface, just to prove the machine is running fine. I see you've got a good
long drive and I wonder if you would just let us run over it for you. No
charge to yourself, of course, guv'nor. You would be doing us a favour.
We'd do it for the price of the materials.*'

Who writes the scripts for these people? The above monologue, delivered this week, was one of the more imaginative, but

they are always good. You can spot the spielers coming a long way off, cruising slowly up the drive in a big pick-up with 'Motorway Maintenance' filling all the spaces where most tradesmen have their names, addresses and telephone numbers.

I never say 'no' before I have heard the spiel, because some of them are works of art, and most performances are worthy of Olivier.

'We are doing the roads for a new estate, and we have too much asphalt for the job. It will go off by tomorrow, go solid in the lorry, so I have to get rid of it this afternoon.

'I don't want to make any money out of this, I just want to clear the lorry, but we'll do you a good job and it's just what your drive needs.'

There must be easier ways to make a living than driving up every drive in sight offering to resurface it. On the other hand, there must be money in it because so many people do it; and the stuff does, literally, fall off the back of lorries.

'Afternoon squire, good to see you again. Last time I was here you said you did not want the drive done, but that was a year ago and it really does need doing now, doesn't it? That's right, squire, I did have a Range Rover last year; but I find this Metro is a good little number. Well, times are hard in the contracting business, just like for farming, eh? I'll be frank, squire, I need the work. So this is what I'll do. I'll do the job for £1.72. Couldn't go lower than that. Well, since we've talked before, and to keep my blokes busy, I'll do it at cost. Just for you, say £1.12. I'll make nothing out of that and . . .'

That is another thing. If ever you do get as far as talking price, you will never get a straight estimate of what the job will cost. They will give you a figure per cubic metre, but who knows whether your pot-holes need ten cubic metres or 100? How many of the cubic metres you pay for actually get on to your drive? And if you don't want to pay cash, forget it.

'I've just come up your drive sir, and if you don't mind me saying so, it's not going to get you through next winter. I've been laying roads for thirty years now sir, and that drive is at breaking point.

'It could crack up in six months, the base will go and you'll have to take the whole thing down six inches and start from scratch. On the other hand, a fresh surface on it now will put another ten years on it. Leave it now, sir, and you will be running into a lot of money. I know drives, sir, take my word for it.'

Not only the script and the actors are Oscar candidates. The casting is always good too – men with honest, open faces, blue eyes or a heavy helping of Irish charm are picked for the starring role of salesman. If you collapse and say 'yes', a gang of very different types arrives to do the work. They operate amazingly fast and disappear before a couple of heavies arrive for the greasy oncers.

'I notice you have had some work done on your drive, but who did it? Tell me who did that for you. That's terrible work there; I'd be ashamed to do work like that. Now here's what I can do to put it right, and if it's not done soon, then all you've spent will have been wasted. What did he charge you for that? Terrible.

'You were robbed, sir, robbed. Well, what I'll do is this. I'll go over all this work for you with a proper surface dressing. Now don't say that, don't be like that. Just because you've had one cowboy here, doesn't mean we are all cowboys. Steady, sir, steady. Don't get excited. You know Lord Somebody, I expect. You don't? Well, he would tell you, sir, what a fine job I do. I've just finished a mile of drive for him.

'Don't call me that, sir. Don't shout. Don't call me a liar, sir. Why don't you believe me?'

Drawing-Room Drips

I shall never forget the Night of the Long Thaw. Like the slow movement in an electronic symphony, the melting ice and snow seeped through the roof in a dozen different places.

GLINK
SPLOT
PLIT, PLIT
BLODGE

The pattern of notes evolved and changed with the filling of the plastic buckets and tin basins positioned beneath the drips; but it was hard to appreciate the subtlety of tone textures and variations because the whole thing started at 2.00 am.

I got to know every crevice and corner of the roof that year as I shovelled away the melting sludge. This year, I resolved to put my knowledge to good use by clearing the snow before the thaw.

Timing, in these matters, is all important; there seemed no point in starting while everything was frozen solid and more snow forecast, yet, on a day when the thermometer never rose anywhere near freezing point . . .

BLIT
DOP
PURP

We had what sounds like the eighteenth-century equivalent of the 1930s lounge lizards: the drawing-room drips.

The only difference between shovelling snow off an eighteenth-century roof and one constructed last year is that in the former case you can tell yourself you are 'conserving the nation's architectural heritage'. It makes the job no easier.

How can there be water splashing indoors when all the morning has been spent trying to persuade outdoor taps to run and troughs to fill?

Obviously the sun streams through the windows and heats the air beneath the roof, melting the bottom layer of snow which immediately trickles off, concealed by its white camouflage canopy, in search of the nearest hole or crack. Result:

TROP

SPLUT etc.

So in the afternoons this week I have forsaken the farm for my little piece of the nation's heritage. After the snow has melted, night falls and freezes it again, producing glaciers six or more inches thick, which clog the valleys on the roof.

Were they real glaciers, they would groan and creak their way towards the downspouts, but the creaking and groaning comes instead from the knees and elbows of the conservation volunteer as he chips away at the ice like some demented cocktail barman, or occasionally strikes lucky and detaches a great dripping sheet of the stuff which can be heaved over the parapet to bounce and shatter on the rock-hard lawn below.

The preferred tool for the job is a kind of burglar's jemmy, spiked and angled at one end, flat at the other. Its drawback is that, used with too much enthusiasm, it will pierce not only the glacier but also the frail roof beneath.

The best tip I've heard this winter for preventing frozen troughs is to stack fresh muck around them. (*Chip, chip, thrust, scrabble* with frozen fingers.)

Perhaps we could cover the whole roof in muck. (*Heave, turn, lean, strain, throw.*)

Why stop there? There must be half an acre up here, could we grow wheat? (What's that? Kind wife below suggesting welcome cup of tea. Sorry about the avalanche. Not a near miss? It looked like a near miss from here.)

Two day later, after further thaw/freeze/thaw cycles, the glaciers have reformed, the moraines have grown again, down-spouts are once more columns of ice . . . but at least we have been spared the ghastly

PLINK

GLUNK

TOCK, TOCK

Only when the real thaw comes shall we know whether we

have also avoided that other bane of life in a heritage situation: the burst pipes.
WHOOSH
SHPURT
PLOOSH

The Rabbit Hunter

Six-thirty on a May morning. Crouching, he moved along the garden wall, brushing the crumbling bricks with his jacket.

The rifle in his hand was comfortably balanced, its carved grip shaped to his cradling fingers as naturally as a chestnut to its shell. Silently, he pushed the old wrought-iron gate ajar and eased his bulk effortlessly through, pleased he had thought to oil the hinges the previous evening. They said the rabbit had got inside the walls because he had not maintained the wire on the bottom of this gate.

They said he was to blame for neglecting the repair, and now there were rabbits inside the walls for the first time in thirty years. Let them say what they like.

Methodically his gaze quartered the terrain. The orchard on the left, the herbaceous border, the rose garden. Nothing. Blackbirds sang. A pigeon flew off the young cabbages. His head ached. The gate was not the only thing a little oiled last night. He planned his route to the peach house.

That is where they said the rabbit had taken up residence . . . right inside the tumble-down peach house, under the water tank.

They said he should have kept the peach house rabbit-proof. They accused him because all the carrots had been nibbled away and the young lettuces decimated.

He thought of all the rabbits elsewhere on the farm; the field behind the village where they had taken out an acre of wheat, where seventy had been shot in one evening with this same rifle.

But that was different. Neither numbers, nor wheat mattered now. This was one rabbit, just him and it, a dawn duel on a May morning. The rabbit's reflexes against the stalker's skill and the bullet's speed. He checked the rifle's smooth safety catch.

Up among the onions something moved. He froze and slowly raised the sight to his right eye. The grey shape was indistinct, blurred by the blossoms of an apple tree. The hairline cross of

the powerful sight wavered and he waited for his arm to stop shivering. It was May in England, after all.

Somewhere out there were sleeping children who last night had read stories about bunnies before they went to bed. Crosspatch gardeners had chased the naughty bunnies with rakes, and the bunnies had had thrilling scrapes and jolly escapes but had always got home to their little burrows.

That was fiction; reality was now; one man against one rabbit. Here the loaded rifle. There the wreck of the carrots. This was the bottom line.

He moved towards a rusted espalier, memory of the time when his garden had been run by three gardeners, when rabbits and pigeons did not dare approach, when even tits, finches and blackbirds were kept at bay by a ring of traps, strings, nets and the old 4.10 in the potting shed.

He used the espalier as a rest, steadying his arm, and raised the rifle a second time.

His training took over. His finger curled round the trigger, his mind took in nothing except the shape quartered by the sight.

Crack. From the onion bed a stone flew flatly into one of the few remaining panes of glass in the peach house and shattered it. In slow, silent, motion, the glass veined and splintered, froze for a second, then slid in shards to the ground. A blackbird flew away from the spot at which he had aimed. Three more pigeons fluttered off the strawberries.

Purposefully, he strode up the path, his view of the onion patch coming clearer. Nothing.

At breakfast, they said that if he did not do something about the rabbit, there would be nothing left in the garden; they reminded him that he had promised last autumn to fix the netting. But he had heard all the words before. It started to rain, a thin, cold drizzle. It was England. In May.

A Woman's Work

Letter to the Editor of the *Daily Telegraph*: 'Sir, Many years ago as a newly married, young commuter, I regularly travelled between Chelmsford and Liverpool Street and I always finished your crossword in the time that journey took; never missing a daily opportunity to smile at my fellow travellers triumphantly as I thrust my *Daily Telegraph* into my briefcase.

'As I no longer use that line I can reveal that my wife, brilliant but insomniac, did the crossword, *in pencil*, before breakfast. I merely had to ensure that I had an ink-filled fountain pen.'

On the day this revealing epistle was published, a letter from the wife of a friend who farms near Chelmsford hit my doormat: '. . . John took the children to Rome during the holidays; I did not feel up to it so stayed at home and played farms,' she writes.

What is it about these Chelmsford wives? Are they exceptional? Imagine feeling 'up to' running the farm but not a trip to Rome . . . is the thought of all that bottom pinching so terrible? Is there no bottom pinching in Chelmsford? Think of the saintly unselfishness of allowing your commuting husband the crossword satisfaction that should by rights be yours.

No. Chelmsford is not unique. All over the country the wife is more than half the team. This is particularly true on a farm and will become an increasingly important part of farm life in the future.

ADAS statistics suggest that the most profitable farms are those run by a family; one tends to think of husky, unpaid sons out there working all hours to bring this paper profitability home, but I suggest the farmer's wife plays a more important role than any other member of the family.

There are not many trades which are a genuine partnership. Of course some of us never say any more about agriculture across the kitchen table than 'there's two with staggers' or 'sprayer's bust', but we are the losers because even wives who don't do the *Telegraph* crossword or turn down trips to Rome can be full of wisdom.

The best advice you can give a young man thinking of going into agriculture is: choose the right wife, for while you are playing farms, she will have to be running the bed and breakfast, doing the cream teas, sorting out the caravan park bookings, selling the free-range eggs, digging the organic potatoes, running the shop, flogging Tupperware.

I cannot decide whether to put 'and' or 'or' between all the items on that list.

There are definitely 'ands' between 'make the beds, cook the dinner, clean the children, feed the dog, save the lambs, answer the telephone, get rid of the rep'.

These routine chores farm wives accept as their lot now, but the need for off-farm income means getting on with the world outside the farm, and who would deny that wives are better at public relations than husbands?

If the only hope for agricultural economic salvation depends on making friends with environmentalists, welfarists and all the other *-ists*, then a woman's work will not stop at the kitchen door, the crossword, the lamb orphanage or wherever its borders now lie. On the farm of tomorrow, it will increasingly be the wife's money that keeps the bank manager quiet.

Wild About Flowers

Like any newcomer to an established social set, I am having trouble sorting out many of the family connections. The Figworts seem particularly inbred, I cannot tell the Cranesbills from the Flaxes, and the Spurges and Cabbages all appear to be cousins by marriage of one another.

My new enthusiasm for wild flowers has made me the butt of much teasing, but I am persevering, and not entirely disinterestedly – there could be money in them yet. The teasers come in two easily identified species: *teaser sempervirens* who thinks I should have known and loved wild flowers since childhood and that I ought to be ashamed of myself; and *joker vulgaris* who believes a real farmer should not be wasting his time on such effeminacies . . . and that I ought to be ashamed of myself.

I feel no shame . . . only ignorance which I am trying to put right with the help of my *Collins Gem Guide*, which is to the Saxifrage family what *Debretts* is to the Marlboroughs. I can now tell you with some confidence that in the last few weeks Lady's Smock and Cowslips have given way to Yellow Irises and Camponi and . . . and . . . and that pinky, pointy thing that grows in the bog.

I did not learn to appreciate wild flowers as a child, because all flowers were cissy and the wild varieties doubly so. There was not room in my adolescent brain for facts about both the newest Austin Healey and Bog Asphodels, and it was the Bog Asphodel that was left out. The *Eagle* and the *Beano* did not give much space to wild flowers and would not have boosted their circulation figures much if they had.

Seamlessly I moved from pre-pubescent ignorance to the ignorance of maturity. Keen to get every ounce of grazing from the water meadows and ton of grain from the higher ground, I treated everything that was not grass or corn as a weed.

It is funny how one's attitude changes. I now find an unbroken green grass meadow boring and treasure the butter-cups which have survived. I am not yet ready to see poppies and marigolds in the wheat, but that day could come. Already, daffodils seem dreary.

I have a problem mapping the border between wild flowers and weeds. Dandelions are in the *Gem Guide*, but I do not find them attractive, and thistles fall into the same category. Brambles, stinging nettles and docks are not listed so I have not got to learn to love them, but cow parsley is my current obsession. Is it pretty? Do I like it? Should I cut it or conserve it?

Those who make fun of my new enthusiasm may yet be forced to stop mocking. If ever I am to prevent the bypass slicing through the farm, it will be because I have found some rare species growing in its path, but there might be money to be had more directly than that. In the Peak District National Park, farmers are paid annual subsidies for the flowers they protect and where National Parks lead, we may yet have to follow.

Of course, all will be ruined if the authorities take hold and we have to start listing Spurges and Worts on our June census forms. While I am looking forward to my first Cowslip Premium cheque, I fear all it will bring with it.

The Secretary General of the Bramble Directorate will send inspectors to check my claim for a grant towards the cost of clearing conifers from my bramble plantation and discover that the same area of land is already being subsidized by the Nettle Conservancy Council.

I maintain that so long as nettles have predominated for five years, I am now entitled to claim the bramble premium but the Brussels directive on the subject is not clear.

If at the same time I fail to fulfil my dandelion quota and become liable for the wild flower super levy, I could be in serious financial hot water, driven beyond the bottle to that well-known white umbellifer, *conium maculatum* ('tall . . . combines purple-spotted stems with a nauseous smell . . .') – hemlock to you and me.

Jopling For Position

Slurryhurst Formulates its Farm Policy

*L*en *Devious (Economics lecturer and newly elected Leader of the Labour Group on Slurryhurst District Council):* Welcome to this inaugural meeting of the Farm Planning Sub. I think we should start by acknowledging the debt we owe to Lord Melchett without whose work, back in 1983, committees such as this would never have come into being. Now the first application is from Slurrypit Farm for a change of policy on thirty acres, switching from winter wheat to spring barley. Comments?

Adrian Broadchalke-Strype (Trainee merchant banker and aspiring Conservative candidate, doing four years on the Council in order to create a good impression at Central Office. Has a weekend cottage in the area): Chairman, my party resents your reference to Lord Melchett. Good planning has been at the core of Conservative thinking for many years and while we place greater emphasis on freedom of the individual than you, we still concede the need for on-going assessments of rural needs within a soundly based economic structure which takes into account contemporary demands for conservation.

Devious: Conservation is not the only criterion. Don't forget the needs of the workers with regard to leisure and recreation. The elitism of a few privileged land-owners traditionally denies the people the right of access to the environmental resources which are properly theirs.

Winifred Wellmeaning (Recently widowed, retired to the country, eager to please): Should we not have a policy of actively discouraging all applications which involve the growing of corn? I saw a television programme only last week about the world's corn surpluses and the way farmers are making millions by growing wheat and barley which no one wants.

Devious: Thank you Councillor Wellmeaning. My party has already established a working group to assess the feasibility of declaring Slurryhurst a grain-free zone.

Broadchalke-Strype: Within what parameters would you then expect agriculture to be conducted?

Wellmeaning: What?

Devious: In view of the Soviet Union's apparently inexhaustible demand for butter, my comrades were considering public support for dairying.

Wellmeaning: Oh no.

Broadchalke-Strype: Of course the economic basis for Soviet butter sales is proven and sound. However you must remember that this is a traditionally arable area and we have no local butter manufacturing capability.

Devious: A grant to the Gay Earth Mothers' Churn Co-operative will solve that problem.

Wellmeaning and Broadchalke-Strype (in unison): Oh no.

Devious: We shall have to defer this decision until policy guidelines have been established. I think the procedure might be that following the formation of a working party and consultancy group we should circulate a discussion document and launch a comprehensive public participation exercise with a view to reporting to Council in one year's time. Good, I see you are all agreed. Until the policy is formed, we'll tell Slurrypit Farm to cease all operations on the thirty acres in question. The next applications are from Great Overdraft Manor, the first seeking permission to switch from a blue tractor policy to green and the second to switch from Herefords to something called Limousins. Does anyone know what colour they are?

Planning officer: A sort of reddish brown, Mr Chairman.

Wellmeaning: As far as the tractors go, I really cannot support green. Somehow green loses its greeniness when seen against the ever-changing panoply of verdant nature which is England in May. Green in winter would be nice, but I always find red a good, strong, spring-time colour. As for the cows, sheep are really so much prettier and they don't frighten the dogs as much as those great big cows. I'm sure the people at the Manor would consider sheep.

Broadchalke-Strype: Limousins sound like immigrants. My party's position on immigrants is perfectly clear; we . . .

At this point your correspondent fell soundly asleep. The meeting continued for a further two hours.

A Load of Rubbish

Fortunately the Prime Minister turned right outside Heathrow when she returned from Japan and made the startling discovery that litter strews the M4 from Hayes to Hammersmith.

Had she turned left, she would have found herself in the country and even more shocked by the rubbish.

'Let me make this perfectly clear, Mr Gladstone. One does not expect to see waste material just dumped in a field like that.'

'But that is my car, Prime Minister.'

'In the field?'

'Yes, Prime Minister. I was trying to get to a trades union meeting in Eastbourne and the car blew up in Horsham. I got home and left it in the field. Unfortunately as I was going through the gate, one of the gate posts jumped out and hit the rear passenger door which accounts for the bend in it. No. The bump on the front wing happened on another occasion. The car was parked in a car park in Aldershot and when I returned to it, there was a crumpled wing marked with yellow paint. Yes, I did consider searching the park for a yellow car but then I thought it might very well be owned by a paratrooper sergeant (it *was* Aldershot) and judged it best to let the matter rest.'

'Serves you right for trying to go to a trades union conference.'

'Yes, Prime Minister.'

'And now that I look more closely, I see it is a French car.'

'Yes, Prime Minister.'

'Serves you right again.'

'We are in the Common Market, Prime Minister, more's the pity.'

'Stop mumbling and listen to me. That wreck in the field is not the only litter on your farm. I have had a small Parliamentary commission studying your patch for some time and the members tell me they have found fertilizer bags in hedgerows, broken troughs and feeders in many of the fields, unidentified pieces of machinery all over the yard, barbed wire trailing from fences, bent gates, lame cattle, fertilizer stripes in the barley, spray burns in the wheat. This is all extremely untidy, Mr Gladstone. It is time you took a grip. We Conservatives offer you self-reliance, a chance to stand on your own feet, low inflation, and Mr Jopling. The Government expects something in return. The least you could do is SMARTEN UP.'

'All farms are like that Prime Minister. They are places where people work. Like factories. Goods come into them, are processed and leave in the form of food. Those goods tend to be wrapped. The processing involves machinery which wears and breaks. Most of these rural factories are a great deal more untidy than this one. We have a more or less permanent bonfire of rubbish going behind the barn and use an old gravel pit as a dump for the larger items. Gypsies come round intermittently and buy scrap from us. To be honest I do not think you will find many farms neater than this.'

'I am not satisfied. My people have approached Bob Geldof and suggested that he spearhead a campaign by this country's wonderful young people aimed at ridding the countryside of litter. He seems amenable. The Saatchi brothers thought he might like to call it *Garbaid*. I find the name a trifle too American but perhaps it will do.'

'Excellent, Prime Minister.'

'Right, that's that one sorted out. Now, what's all this about Salt 2? I wonder if Mick Jagger would take that on?'

Busy Doing Nothing

Could Prince Charles and Michael Jopling be Zen Buddhists? It would explain a lot of things, including the choice of the high and silent places of the Lake District for the recent meeting of European farm Ministers, the Prince's presence at that meeting, and, most of all, Mr Jopling's belief in the fallowing of the land, as advocated in his cereals set-aside policy.

I am indebted to a reader for sending me the lengthy cutting from the *Times of India* which triggered this transcendent flash of

understanding. It is a review of *The One-Straw Revolution: An Introduction To Natural Farming* by Masanobu Fukuoka, published by the Friends Rural Centre, Rasulia, Madhya Pradesh, price thirty rupees.

You have not read it yet? Send away while stocks last. Natural farming is set to sweep Europe.

'The author studied plant pathology and was working for the Yokohama Customs Bureau inspecting incoming and outgoing plants for disease-carrying insects,' the *Times of India* reviewer writes.

'One May morning at the age of twenty-five he had a strange experience which revolutionized his life. He realized in a flash, as it were, that man knows nothing at all, that there is no intrinsic value in anything, that every action is futile and every effort meaningless, and that he himself understood nothing.' The next day he resigned.

You get that feeling often?

Secure in the Zen realization that 'form is emptiness and emptiness is form', Mr Fukuoka set out to be a 'do-nothing farmer', an approach to agriculture described by his Lake District followers as a 'set-aside policy'.

'What about not doing this and not doing that?' Mr Fukuoka asked himself, very much in the manner of Mr Jopling. Mr F. has neither ploughed, weeded nor fertilized his farm for twenty-five years and now he has the answer to his questions – record rice yields of up to twenty-two bushels per acre, which is a great deal more than they can get in the Lake District even in the wettest summer.

Non-cultivation is as fundamental to natural farming as it is to set-aside. The earth 'cultivates itself naturally by means of penetration of plant roots and the activity of micro-organisms, small animals and earthworms,' Mr F. writes. All you have to do is watch it.

Will do-nothing farming appeal to the Europeans? Has anyone discussed its implications with Denmark's micro-organisms and Spain's siesta-loving earthworms? Did the Prince and the Minister get the Zen message across? Will the cardinals, bishops and archimandrites oppose the spread of this rival religion?

It was obviously significant that the Ministers were hurried out of the country before Harvest Festival Sunday. They could hardly have stood shoulder to shoulder in Bowness church and praised the Lord because 'the pastures are clothed with flocks; the valleys also are covered over with corn.'

Such sentiments are as out of date as the language of the King James Bible.

No. 'Do nothing' is the cry, every action futile, every effort meaningless. Only one puzzle remains. When Mr Fukuoka saw the light and realized this, that May morning long ago in the Yokohoma customs shed, his immediate reaction was to resign. But Mr Jopling?

Something to Sing About

I t cannot only be because nothing rhymes with Jopling that no good songs are written about British farming.

In the United States, a host of stars rallied round for the Farm Aid concert and raised money for farmers facing bankruptcy, but it is hard to imagine Wembley filling up for a British equivalent – and I suspect the blame must lie with the lyric writers.

Whenever a song is about farming it is mocking. Remember the Wurzels' *'Brand New Combine Harvester'*? It struck me as the height of tender, loving affection to offer the girl of your dreams the key to your combine, but the Wurzels always got laughs out of it.

American songwriters make corn country and cattle lands seem romantic; but then they even make their road system sound romantic. American lyrics make farmers seem as macho as truckers. Why does 'stockman' sound less hairy-chested than 'cowhand'? Why is it that 'Norfolk' or 'Exeter' does not conjure up the image of big country freedom and man taming nature that singers squeeze out of 'Wyoming' or 'Albuquerque'?

Why does 'Route 66' or 'Highway One' sound so much more thrilling than 'A1(M)' or 'West Country Holiday Route (Light Vehicles Only) No Overtaking'? Why is 'Marlboro Country' as different from 'Marlborough Country' as hand-tooled boots from green wellies?

The difference starts at the title. The Wurzels' *'Middle for Diddle'* and *'Down in Nempnett Thrubwell'* just do not hit you in the same place as Springsteen's *'Highway Patrolman'* or *'Downbound Train'*.

If Springsteen or Dylan were let loose on the farmland of Britain, could he heal our tattered image? With Tina Turner on our side, could we make stubble burning acceptable, or even a kind of challenge to our masculinity (whatever that means).

I am only a little heartened by the news that Andrew Lloyd Webber is about to take possession of a large Hampshire dairy and arable farm. Could it be that Evita, Cats and all his other smashes will be followed by the greatest rural musical since Annie Get Your Gun, or will even he find the problems with exciting lyrics insurmountable?

Just thinking of a snappy title is hard enough. 'Hagberg' is topical. So is 'Outgoers Scheme'. But you cannot quite see either of those in lights in Shaftesbury Avenue (shortly transferring to Broadway).

Sorry Mr Lloyd Webber, I cannot help with the title but I have been down to the library and consulted a rhyming dictionary on the subject of Jopling. Free and for nothing I offer your lyricist the following.

'Hoppling' which means 'tying the feet together'.

'Toppling' which means 'falling forwards'.

And 'Stoppling' which means 'closing with a bung or plug'.

All three seem strangely apt, don't they?

The Grapes of Wrath

We had the terrible story of Naboth's vineyard in church the other day. It struck me as an Old Testament tale about a compulsory purchase order, but that is possibly because compulsory purchase orders have been rather on my mind since the engineers for the bypass came to call.

Ahab, you remember, coveted Naboth's vineyard which he wanted to turn into a herb garden – a sort of ninth century BC alternative enterprise. No quota on thyme; nasty surplus of Israeli grapes.

The king offered an exchange or outright purchase for cash, but Naboth refused to part with the land on the grounds that it had been in the family for generations.

Ahab fell into an unregal sulk, lay in his bed and refused to eat. Enter his wife, Jezebel, who tells him not to be so pathetic and by a ruse involving forged letters, false witnesses and a trumped-up charge neatly gets to grips with the situation and arranges for Naboth to be stoned to death.

Obviously his solicitor had fallen down on the job, because Naboth seems to have died intestate, leaving the way clear for the king to claim the vineyard as his own, which he lost no time in doing.

The Lord, however, had strong views on compulsory purchase even by kings, and I see no reason why he should not apply similarly harsh standards today to the Department of Transport. The Ahab/Jezebel gang of two was sentenced to death by the Lord, their bodies to be eaten by the dogs. Quite right too.

At the last minute, Ahab squirmed out of his punishment by rending his clothes, dressing in sackcloth and fasting, but I do not see why any contemporary civil servant should be able to avoid divine retribution so easily. Times being what they are, he would find himself a designer sackcloth outfit; and the fast would be no more than ten days in a health farm.

Perhaps if the Lord had not weakened, if Ahab really had suffered all that he threatened, compulsory purchase would never have survived beyond Old Testament times. I have never quite understood the particular punishment handed out to Ahab in addition to the death sentence (it is not available to our local magistrates for dealing with straw burning offences or speeding, for example) but I Kings 21 makes it seem a sure deterrent to almost anything:

'I will bring evil upon thee and will take away thy posterity and will cut off from Ahab him that pisseth against the wall . . .'

There, as they say, you have it. That is what it is all about, squire.

CPOs survived through history in spite of this precedent. Henry VIII was obviously not swayed by it when the monasteries got above themselves, but you would think that once parliamentary procedures had taken over from monarchical whim, compulsory purchase might be one of the first things to be done away with.

No such luck. I suppose that when the documents come through my letter box I shall find out what year the current CPO laws were made, and I must face the fact that no road, railway or canal would ever have been built without them.

All the same, 'In a free society no purchase by the state should ever be compulsory' would make a good sixth form debating motion, bearing in mind that everything and everyone has a price. Naboth told Ahab: 'The Lord forbid it me that I should give the inheritance of my fathers unto thee.'

Unsubtly, Ahab missed the point here. I believe Naboth was opening negotiations with an invitation to bargain. *Giving* inheritance is one thing, but *selling* it (presumably for a great deal more than Ahab had offered) would be quite another. Jezreel property prices might well have been booming at the time, who knows?

Obviously CPOs save the authorities millions of pounds, but they will bring terrible retribution on the under- and permanent secretaries responsible. They face an awful lot of trouble with their posterity and him that pisseth against the wall.

Menopausal Man Sweats It Out

AS THE YEARS TAKE THEIR TOLL,
THE FARMER STRUGGLES IN THE IRON GRIP OF A

Facing Forty With a Fork

Thoughts of Jane Fonda's body occupied my mind through most of the two weeks spent rearranging grass on the silage clamp this year.

Do not misunderstand. You would have to be very weird to find anything romantic about a silage clamp in the middle of a hot and humid afternoon. No, it was nothing more wicked than money which led my wandering thoughts towards lithe Jane.

She is currently making a small fortune out of a chain of exercise centres where people pay to be made to sweat and ache. 'When exercising,' she says, 'you must feel the muscles burn. The pain is the proof.' And 3,200 people a week in Beverly Hills pay $7 each a session to feel the burn and pain.

'Think,' I thought, as the pitchfork plunged into another wedge of grass, 'of all that energy going to waste.'

'Consider,' I considered, while another green hill tumbled off the back of the buckrake, 'how the straining and heaving might be applied to moving this stuff around.'

'Ponder,' I pondered, as the trailer roared into the yard with another ton or two of not-very-dry matter, 'the fact that people will actually pay to sweat. What has Beverly Hills got that the Lambourn Downs have not?'

Further research reveals that dear Jane is on to a good thing because aerobic dancing is now taking over from jogging as the trendy way to keep fit.

You might find this hard to believe if you have tried to drive down Piccadilly lately, impeded on all sides by puffing, perspiring figures crossing from Green Park to Hyde Park and back, but California – and, soon, Berkshire – sets trends which London follows.

I do not really know what aerobic dancing is, but imagine it is not very different to the average Scottish reel; and the thinking behind it appears to be similar to the philosophy that gets middle-aged men in Scottish regiments on to the parade ground for half an hour of foursomes and eightsomes before breakfast.

So what about aerobic silage making? For $7 an hour – okay, to you, as an introductory offer, because I like your face, call it $6.50 – you can come and indulge in spasms of intensive activity with a pitchfork, all set to the rhythmic roar of a tractor at full throttle belting up the clamp towards you with buckrake lowered like an array of chef's skewers heading for you – the shish kebabs.

It keeps you on your toes.

Leotards are frowned upon, but this year, for the first time in memory, the sun was so hot that the smell of sun-tan oil mingled with the usual silage-time aromas of diesel, fermenting grass and hydraulic fluid.

'What additive did you use this year, old boy?' 'I rather fancy Ambre Solaire.'

Jane's body is forty-four years old, five years older than mine, and I have to admit that even the most cursory comparison of the two will show that aerobic dancing is a more effective streamliner than aerobic silage making. However, that is only because the whole thing has not been properly presented.

You will have noticed from television commercials that Mark McCormack is doing a wonderful job for Angela Rippon, who has given her name to something very like aerobic dancing except that you do it, as they say, 'in the privacy of your own home'. A book of instructions and a record are all you need to lose fat as fast as a Friesian in February.

So I am putting together some of my best loved Scottish dance tunes and a booklet called *Facing Forty with a Fork*. I guarantee plenty of pain. I just want Mark and Angela to get to work on it and we'll be in business. Can't you see it?

'Darling, I'm off to this wonderful farm where you spend all day out in the sun, positively surrounded by fresh-cut grass, throwing it around. Your muscles just shriek after a day or two, but it is all in a good cause because you are doing wonders for yourself and you are making sure all those poor old cows have something to eat in winter. Isn't it exciting?

'And there is this nice man who runs the farm, who takes your money. He says he is saving up to go to a fitness class himself. In Beverly Hills. With Jane Fonda.'

The Why Factor

S he is blonde and pretty and they call her Sammy. She looked me straight in the eye and asked: 'Why did you become a farmer?'

She cannot be more than twelve years old, one of a group of five from a local primary school who came to quiz me for information to be fed into something called the BBC Domesday Report. Already they had given me stick for having an electric fence beside a public right of way and their delightful headmaster had come to my rescue by suggesting, only partly in jest, that it might be there to keep children out of fields as well as stock in them.

And now Sammy. Had she any idea what an effect she had? Why did I, back in the mists of time before she was born, become a farmer? Through her bright and innocent eyes it obviously seemed a daft way to try to make a living.

She had learned in the course of the interview that everything I produced was in surplus; that I did not get a regular pay cheque like her Dad; that crops, sheep and cattle get diseases; and that the weather can be a serious headache.

Once upon a time, Sammy my love, when the world was young, farming seemed to be a useful way to make a living; now, the best thing about it from a little girl's point of view is that you can keep a pony.

I must have decided to become a farmer one May evening when the sky was clear, interest rates in single figures and milk in short supply. Was there ever such a time? Has middle age already brought an unreal rosy glow to the 1960s?

Sammy was only the first visitor of the week; hot on her heels came a coach party of twenty-five Americans. It is a couple of years since we went into the lunches-for-Americans trade. Each group is as charming as the last and, since they all seem to come from New England, as different from the Dynasty/Dallas stereotype as the Queen Mother is from Nancy Reagan.

They oohed and aahed over the untreated Channel Island cream which my wife dollops up with the strawberries. After I had assured the man I was serving that it would not cause an immediate coronary – although it possibly should carry a government health warning – the conversation somehow swung from cream to milk to quotas.

We all know how much US farmers are suffering, but the idea of an artificial limit on production struck him as a completely unacceptable restriction on trade. 'Why don't you quit milk?' he said. Coming so soon after Sammy's 'Why did you become a farmer' his question left me spluttering. I knew there was some excellent reason, but faced by his incredulity, my brain crunched, stripped a cog or two and completely failed to engage.

Nor is that all. I am writing this on the eve of a visit by a local Young Farmers' club. I never was a Young Farmer (or a young farmer, come to that) but I have a fair idea what I am in for and I am dreading it.

They will be energetic, enthusiastic, knowledgeable, primed by their college teachers to ask all kinds of questions about wheat diseases and application rates for fungicides, soil types and seed rates, grass varieties and weed names. Again, the mental gearbox will graunch and jam and their keen, inquiring minds will leave me floundering.

Sammy and the American will swim in the ether before my eyes. One will ask why I ever got into this line of business and the other will ask why I do not get out. Faced by such ingenuousness I shall dive into a welcoming pool of nostalgia, mumble about how straightforward and good farm life used to be and come up gasping. Or, possibly, go under for the third time.

Lifting Bales is Hot, Hard Work

'Why am I lifting hay bales,' he thought, 'when I could be rowing the Atlantic or walking across the Sahara?'

He glanced hopefully at the sky, searching for a cloud, but the sunshine was unrelenting, merciless. Sweat pricked his eyes; his back threatened extra-parliamentary action; his arms were as keen to work as an Arthur Scargill picket; his shoulders protested like twin Tariq Alis.

He was forty years old now, a responsible family man; was it right to risk orphaning two growing boys? Was the life insurance up to date? His mind began to drift.

Six years previously he had written a piece in *Big Farm Weekly* decrying big bales on the grounds that the whole farm system had to be reorganized to accommodate them. 'The conventional bale seems to be an ideal size and weight,' he had written then.

But six years previously he had been six years younger, six years fitter, six years lighter! Or possibly, it was just that hay was six years lighter, for it is a fact that hay gets heavier every year.

True, lifting bales then had been hot, hard work; but filling the barn had seemed so straightforward that he had even sold and not replaced the aged elevator. Now, as *Daily Mail* subs composed headlines about 'sunburnt Britain', and keen reporters made the most of the fact that it was hotter in Scunthorpe than Sitges, he found himself doing the elevating with his own two hands.

In his par-boiled brain, strange fantasies steamed. 'The trouble is,' he thought, 'that the more bales you take off this trailer, the lower the load gets and the higher the stack gets, thereby steadily increasing the amount of lift you have to give each succeeding layer of bales.

'What's needed is a system of filling the barn from the top. Or unloading the trailer from the bottom.

'What's needed is a computer and instant recall of the "O" Level physics syllabus. Careful study of weights and leverages, forces and angles, should minimize the amount of effort expended. And every fraction of a joule saved is inestimably valuable.

'At this rate, things could get serious. There might not be strength remaining by seven o'clock with which to raise a glass and start replenishing all this liquid that seems to be flowing from every pore.'

He started searching despairingly for reasons to put off the lifting of the next bale by even a few seconds. He bent to study the strings like Precious Mackenzie psyching out the lifting bar. Meticulously he lifted a stray leaf from the bales, brushed loose hay from the twine; only then did he bend and take the strain.

It was best when his partner in the barn had something to say . . . a stop . . . a talk . . . perhaps even a few minutes to sit on the bales. With luck a rep would call, or a thunderstorm break, or any drama major enough to slow the rhythm of lifting and heaving, lifting and heaving.

Next year he'll be forty-one; next year he'll mechanize; eat his words about big bales; perhaps cut out hay altogether; switch to big bales of treated straw, untouched by hand.

The heat can do strange things to a man. As he sat in the evening, writing his piece for *Big Farm Weekly*, he could hear the mower's distinctive whine in the distance. What had possessed him to shut up the silage aftermath for some soft, late hay?

He could smell the fresh-cut grass. 'We might get an extra 800 bales out of that' he thought, and enjoyed the prospect, until a spasm gripped him across the bottom of his back and painfully reminded him what 800 bales entailed.

Weight of Opinion

I first suspected the Luddites were right when a friend told me that three of his men were spending the evenings lifting weights at the local health club. Farmworkers lifting weights for recreation? Hernias and slipped discs, where are the sixteen-stone sacks of yesteryear?

I knew for sure that mechanization had gone too far the last time I went skiing. Discussing life with my legs in the evenings, they maintained that they were unprepared for the amount of use to which they were suddenly and violently being put and threatened industrial action – a walk-out to be precise.

Getting me from desk to Land Rover does not tax them much, so I had to concede that I had not properly prepared them for the perils of the powder and the pressures of the piste. I promised them that they would never again be sent into battle so ill-equipped in calf and thigh.

So it came about that two months ago I plucked up my courage, swallowed my pride and walked into my local health club, which happens to be less than a mile from my front door; and there I was initiated into the strange world of the Nautilus machine and introduced to the dim sub-cultures of body-builders and weight-lifters.

Three kinds of people use the club. There are those like myself, clinging by their fingertips to an illusion of youth, struggling round a gentle, weight-training circuit. There are those who aspire to be Mr Universe. And there are the men who roar and grunt to lift more kilograms than I can count – only to put them down again.

The middle-aged keep-fitters work their way round a succession of Nautilus machines, each one designed to exercise a separate group of muscles, which would have brought a sparkle to the eye of the lads who organized the Spanish inquisition.

Here you lie on your back and push with your legs; there you squeeze between the chains and pulleys and lift things above your head; on this one you lie on your side, hook your legs round a lever and make yourself look a complete idiot.

To be truthful, you look a bit of a nit from start to finish. 'Is there anyone there punier than you, Dad?' asked younger son perceptively. 'No,' I admitted. 'Not even the women.'

The real professionals reject the orthodox way of fitting themselves into the terrible machines and devise all sorts of alternatives designed to make the job of lifting a couple of hundred kilograms as difficult as possible. They straddle the apparatus and do their best to rip it apart, whereas I approach it timidly and use it respectfully in case something slips and puts me off skiing for life. These instruments of pain and suffering, like the rack, are bigger and stronger than I.

The body-builders work on bits of their bodies as if they were moulding plasticine. 'Triceps today then, Kev?' 'No, they are getting well out of proportion. I'm giving the lats a couple of sessions.'

Lats? These boys have muscles where I don't even get goose pimples and they discuss their shape in the way the judges assess carcases at Smithfield.

The third group, the weight-lifters, are less beautiful and more terrifying. They spend long periods doing nothing but prowl. There is one in particular, whom I have christened Desperate Dan because he looks surprisingly like my boyhood comic strip favourite, he of the cow pie and stubbled chin.

Dan lifts massive weights and concentrates so hard on the problem before doing so that his eyes cross. I may be wrong, but I don't think either body-builders or weight-lifters have to take intelligence tests before going to work. All right: neither do middle-aged skiers.

The final lure of the health club is the unisex Jacuzzi, a pleasure I have not been brave enough to sample. 'Having a jacuzzi today then?' Kev asked his mate on my first visit. 'Hang on, let's look,' his mate replied, peering round the door which leads to this mysterious pool of delights. 'Yeah,' he came back, 'Jeanette's in there today,' and both the lads grabbed their towels.

Two days later, Dan was considering the same thing. He too peered round the door, turned back, and told his friend: 'It's Bust in there.' This I had to see. A lady body-builder with a nickname like that must be worth seeing. My fevered imagination had overheated, however. What Dan meant was that the Jacuzzi was broken.

The Townies Are Coming

AN UNFAMILIAR CASTE OF PERSON COMES OUT OF
THE CITIES TO DISTURB THE RUSTIC TRANQUILLITY

The Woodburning Stove Threat

There is a new threat to the fast-diminishing woodland of the home counties – wood-burning stoves. Strange cast-iron contrivances have invaded English homes from Stevenage to Staines, from Southend to Sevenoaks, and driven the traditional grate on to the rubbish dump, where it joins coal-scuttles, fenders, toasting forks, and all the other impedimenta of open coal fires.

The result is that from first light to gloaming, Saturdays and Sundays in the Shires are suffused with the irritated roar of power-saws and the crash of timber. On Mondays, City offices buzz not with the price of copper futures or the horrors of the money supply, but with tales of newly discovered sources of oak and still undiscovered hoards of beech.

Tips on the proper use of wedges are swapped on the Stock Exchange for the .names of shops that sell saw chains on

Saturday afternoons, and the boasting at lunchtime at Lloyds is of tons chopped and cordwood stacked rather than birdies achieved or trout landed.

No tree is safe. Last week a large limb which crashed off an old beech near a footpath behind the farm here had been sawn up and loaded into a Volvo Estate almost before it hit the ground . . . certainly long before I got around to doing anything about it.

The telephone and door bells ring regularly with people asking what timber I can spare, and although our woods are as full of the dead and dying as a Scutari ward, I cannot meet the insatiable demand. The trees just do not die fast enough . . . with the result that one desperate Stokoften owner has proposed cutting down a particularly attractive living ash and turning it into logs.

'Ash burns so well,' he said, rather confusingly.

You can tell the hard-bitten City lumberjack by the look in his eye. He is as single-minded as an Arthurian knight with only a rather mangy dragon between him and the Holy Grail.

He prowls around the unsuspecting tree with the cold calculation of a cat with a half-dead mouse; finally his hand reaches for the chain-saw starter cord; the beast howls into life, screams a couple of times as he twitches the trigger, and settles into a steady roar as the blade starts to sink into the timber.

I imagine my distant relative, W. E. Gladstone, derived the same satisfaction from his favourite relaxation as these latter-day winter fuel merchants get from theirs. For the Prime Minister used to rid himself of the cares of Westminster by chopping down trees on his estate in Flint.

Whereas he, perhaps, envisaged Disraeli before him as he swung his axe, today's power-saw experts picture union leaders, bank managers and the Ayahtollah.

Of all the scores of dead elms we have been faced with, now only one remains. Until a few weeks ago there were two real giants which had proved more than a match for the hard-bitten men who must work all week to feed their families and all weekend to feed their Potbellies.

I used to show the two daunting monsters and say casually: 'You can have one of them if you want.' It worked until one particularly expert executive said: 'Lend me the tractor and a wire rope for the day and I'll have it.' He did.

Now I'm left with one twelve-foot-diameter colossus, brooding over a field of winter wheat like a vulture on a carcase.

It is all sour grapes, of course. Those of us with open fires and

oil-burning, unpatriotic, central heating boilers are still misera-
bly playing the shivering game – he who can longest delay the
lighting of the boiler, wins. At these latitudes, there is general
agreement that if you can manage with no central heating until
now – December – you are first division material. Relegation
faces those who go too far and find burst pipes in radiators or
are sued for divorce by wives with chilblains.

A certain amount of cheating is permitted. Electric blankets,
strategically placed fan heaters, interlocking underwear, all help
the circulation, but they do not prevent the rising damp turning
the floorboards green in the corners of disused dining rooms.

I wonder if the Arabs know what they have done to England's
floorboards – and our woodlands.

Do you think green floorboards would burn well?

Forgettable Characters You May Have Met

S urvived. This is the time of year when farmers' heads come
up off their chests, their eyes lift from the slurry around them
and life begins to seem worth living again.

Against all the odds, the grass is growing, we have not
destroyed all eco-systems with our too-strong chemicals and too-
large machines; spring is not entirely silent. Animals have
survived the winter, some have even multiplied, and crops have
put down roots and thrust up shoots. Sap has risen – as it always
has – in the trees and hedgerows. The end is not yet nigh,
perhaps.

The effect of the season undoubtedly plays a part in the
transformation that creeps over the farming community in April.
People who were ready to retire in February are suddenly
bursting with plans and schemes, full of ambitions, charged with
confidence that this will be the year they join the ten-tonne club
AND stop serving double faults on the tennis court.

Have you met the man who just before Christmas met
someone whose brother worked in the City and had told him
over lunch at the Turf Club that MLR would never come down?

The poor fellow believed it, and all through January, February and March he invested heavily in claret, which he reckoned
he was getting cheap from a company in Deptford which accepts
Access cards. He became the sole and founder member of the
MCL Club – the More Claret at Lunchtime Club – and took to
sampling a bottle daily between the hours of 12.30 and 2.00.

'MCL not MLR' he was heard muttering one day while shooting, during the brief hour or two of gloom which passes for afternoon in December; and he convinced himself that the iron in the wine was good for his back, particularly if said back was placed in a horizontal position for an hour or two every evening at about five o'clock.

The MCL Club folded up a couple of weeks ago, because the clocks had changed and the Club's member rediscovered evenings. He also realized that during his snoring hibernation somebody had done something or other about MLR. He neither knows nor cares Howe or why; he is too excited by the prospect of yet another approach to his bank manager.

Perhaps you have come across that man who is always on the point of emigrating . . . has been for years. He spends winter evenings studying land prices in Australia, the potential of circle farms in Texas, sheep systems in New Zealand, the political situation in East Africa.

He just wants to farm somewhere where there is not much mud. He has grown to hate putting on and taking off his gumboots a dozen times a day; he is convinced that British bureaucracy is the most pervasive in the world, that Mrs

Thatcher is showing dangerous Socialist tendencies, that he can never be either free or warm in England again.

The future is all worked out; with the proceeds of the sale of his Gloucestershire hectares he can buy thousands of acres near Goomalling or a nice fruit farm outside Hobart.

Funny thing is, it's April and he's still here, spreading nitrogen like there was no tomorrow, planning rotations for the next ten years.

Another character you might have met is the arable man who always shortens his winter by spending three weeks in the West Indies with a lot of racehorse trainers who traditionally go there while waiting for the flat season to start. I suppose it is fortunate people like him who drive us livestock slaves to think of booze and emigration; for us there is no escape from the climate, no chance to swap rheum for rum in February.

Terrible isn't it? Perhaps I should come clean and tell you that when you read this I shall be just returning from two weeks' suffering and misery in the Alps ... not so much claret at lunchtime as *vin ordinaire*, but very tasty none the less.

Mixing with Money

It has come to the attention of the management that some of you are secret subscribers to strange underground newsletters, sent to you under plain wrapper to enjoy in the privacy of your own home.

The cause of these moral lapses is the Prime Minister and her loose talk of a share-owning democracy. Her corrupting influence has led many honest farmers to believe that money is to be made more easily on the streets of the City of London than in their own fields.

In response to these ill-suppressed yearnings, I now proudly present farming's financial section.

It is based on the most thorough research. Twice in the last few weeks, I have put on my grubby raincoat and ventured on to the sleazy pavements of the Square Mile.

First stop was the directors' dining room of a major merchant bank. Only a few years ago, lunch here was a daily orgy. You were asked for 12.30 and it was strongly recommended that you kept the afternoon free. Brandy followed claret which followed a light Sancerre which followed a heavy gin and tonic.

This time, the whole meal was over before you could say

'intangible assets'. Tomato juice, Perrier water, grilled sardines and everyone was back at their desks by 2.15. Old friends who once admitted freely that they worked a fifteen-hour week were boasting – BOASTING – of being workaholics, never home before 7.30.

Their only explanation for this awful change was a muttered reference to something called the Big Bang. I could but take a straw from my hair and suck knowledgeably upon it, for I did not know what they meant.

Undeterred, a few days later I set out again to renew my low life contacts. This time, a humble stockbroker was my target.

Have you seen how these people live? I don't suppose my man was on less than £40,000 a year but at the wine bar where he chose to entertain me, there was hardly room for his wallet. Housed sheep require one square metre of space per ewe. Feeding stockbrokers survive with a great deal less.

I came clean and admitted that I often felt inadequate when discussing economics because I did not understand the words. He leant as close to my ear as the bulge of credit cards in his breast pocket would allow and said: 'Nobody does.'

Then he came up with the one really solid piece of advice that has come out of my research, and I pass it on to you gladly.

When the conversation lightly turns to supply-side deficits, Reagonomics, the prospects for the Yen or the merits of the European currency snake, just say: 'Come now: surely it all depends on M3?'

This is not the M3 that runs from London to Basingstoke. This is the M3 that is supposed to measure or predict the rate of inflation, but which is so complex that, from Yale to Yokohama, computers hum day-and-night in an endless struggle to get it right.

Adjusting the binder twine knotted nattily below the knee of the trousers of my church- and market-suit, I thanked him for his advice and swapped the foetid air of the wine bar for the roaring noise of the City street.

'M3 and the Big Bang,' I muttered to myself as I made my way home and I confess to a sinful delight in the thrill of being part of this secret world, if only for a lunchtime.

Now I understand the cravings and desires that you find so hard to suppress. You want to get rich, to ride M3 and the Big Bang.

So, now, do I. Once you have tasted the decadent pleasures of high finance, even the thrill of a new fertilizer programme somehow leaves you unfulfilled.

Read on then, and feel no guilt. Leading therapists agree that there is no harm in believing that somewhere out there is a system, consultant, newsletter, position or adviser that can sort out your financial hang-ups and leave you limp but happy.

Brought to Book

As the last chance of a summer holiday recedes into the rain clouds, with it disappears the farmer's annual opportunity to pretend to culture and . . . read a book.

Smug city folk are even now returning from the Mediterranean, Mumbles or Malibu, ready to bore for Europe on the subject of 'this wonderful book which you must not miss'.

Do not feel put down or intellectually threatened by these literary poseurs. You can pose with the best of them with a little help from this *Instant Guide to Today's Countryside Best Sellers:*

The Jopling Factor by Len Devious. Kremlinpress. £9.99. A chilling look into a future Britain in which the peasants have risen against the NFU/MAFF/Conservative Party cartel and smashed the Government. The hero is young Arthur Scargale, gritty son of the Islington soil who rises to become president for life of the People's Buccleuch Collective Farms, the giant co-operative which takes over the estates previously owned by the country's largest landowner. The description of the Nicaraguan landing in Dumfriesshire is particularly convincing.

Farmofax. Farmofaxpress. £99.99. All Gloucestershire is raving about this absolutely indispensable essential which is on every agricultural executive's desk from Cheltenham to Cirencester. In just one 599-page, loose-leaf, leather-bound, gold-embossed volume you get: the date and month of EVERY DAY in the year; full details of Bank Holidays, high tides, licensing hours and the time of Sunday Evensong in the English Church in EVERY CAPITAL CITY in Europe; names, addresses and telephone numbers of all major Jacuzzi suppliers in Western Australia; a map of the London Underground; the up-to-date list of best Test innings by British batsmen since 1983; pull-out centrefold full-colour picture of Torvill and Dean with the complete score of Ravel's Bolero, hand-lettered on antique rice paper; special, personalized spaces in which YOU can record YOUR VERY OWN VAT number, accountant's address and latest, up-to-the-moment, computerized OVERDRAFT FIGURE.

The Fascist Farmer's Guide to Straw Burning. Swastikapress. £12.77. Winner of this year's Hedge-Grubbers Conservation Award, this informative little volume points out all the loopholes in the straw-burning regulations and includes several valuable tips on how to present your defence to the magistrates. Its companion volume, *The Fascist Farmer's Guide to Tree Felling*, has helped many land owners get round Tree Preservation Orders. (Now in preparation: *The Fascist Farmer's Guide to SSSIs.*)

So You Want To Be a Farmer. Shirley Williamspress. £10.10. Latest in this famous educational publishing house's careers series. A convincing case is made against the destruction of our environmental heritage by the struggle to produce unwanted food. Perhaps the title page says it all. It reads: 'So You Want To Be A Farmer? Forget it.'

So You Want To Be A Duke? Stocktonpress. £110.00. A reprint of this classic nineteenth-century guide to the clamber up the social ladder from obscurity to a Dukedom and 15,000 acres.

Hunt Balls and Shooting Parties by Amanda and Reginald Broadchalke-Strype. Tatlerpress. 25 guineas. They say they still blush in Leicestershire whenever this bitchy, witty book is mentioned. Referred to in three divorce cases already, it does for Market Harborough what Dallas did for Dallas.

The Writing's on the Wall

Sign writing would be a profitable side line. I have just come back from the farm in Galloway, a part of the world that has had to embrace tourism and alternative farm enterprises, and the token of that embrace is the proliferation of signs.

Farms in Galloway tend to be at the end of long tracks. Where the track joins the main road is called the road en', and used to be marked by no more than a simple metal sign bearing the name of the holding.

When I was a child the road en' was an important meeting point and transit station. The bus driver, for instance, would throw out the sausages from the butcher at our road en', and we would walk down to pick them up before the collie found them.

Now the road en' is more an advertising site than a *post restante*, and the simple metal signs have been replaced by boards proclaiming to the car-loads of passing tourists what is on offer at the far end of the various farm roads and tracks. Between the farm and the local town I saw two *Routiers* signs. *Routiers* in

Kirkcudbrightshire! Whatever next? *Bateaux mouches* on the Nith? The *tricolour* fluttering above Burns' monument?

There seems to be nothing which is not a potential tourist attraction. The official leaflet about the cliff walk which runs across my land even describes the prospect of a chance meeting with a sun-bathing adder as if it were a come-on.

Should I advertise adders at my road en'? Currently it is one of the few in the area which still boasts no more than a straightforward name, but then it leads to one of the only farms left producing milk in a parish where once the tanker – or the churn lorry – trundled down every track.

The fact that we are still farming should not preclude us from cashing in on the tourist trade. There is a farm not far away which numbers among its attractions 'hill cattle, Blackface sheep, working dogs, and dyking'. Would people pay to see our only marginally less mundane 'silage clamps, slurry tanks, calves, collies, and Friesians'? I honestly think that if we painted the sign big enough, they would.

You can tell that an area has become popular with tourists, or 'visitors' as they politely call them in Galloway, when everything has become a craft. All crafts, however hideous the product, are thought to be attractive. I wonder why people buy on holiday things from which they would run a mile during the rest of the year.

The signs shriek: Horncraft. Walking sticks. Sheepskins. Pottery. Gemrocks. Clogs. Engraved Glass. All have become so desirable that the go-ahead local tourist board has been able to devise a Galloway Craft Trail, the car-borne craft addicts' equivalent of a pub crawl.

Other signs proclaim arts festivals in towns where not long ago Art was the name of the local Bingo caller, and no council can hold its head up in public until it has sponsored a 'civic week' or two.

Any collection of pitchforks and turnip shredders becomes a 'Museum of Rural/Farm/Local Life', and perfectly ordinary pursuits such as shopping, walking, golfing, sailing, eating and drinking tea become tourist board boasts . . . draws almost as splendid as that perennial attraction to beat all attractions: 'FREE TOILETS'.

But what you really need if you are to pull in the public is a ruin. Galloway is rich in ruins – abbeys and castles which I would classify as serious ruins, little keeps and watch-towers which in some cases are just heaps of stones, and agriculture which may yet be the ruin of us all.

All this could be combined in the perfect road en' sign: VISIT MEIKLE GRANTS FARM. SEE THE RUINED FARMER DRINK TRADITIONAL SCOTS WHISKY AND KICK HERITAGE COWS. WATCH THE ANCIENT CRAFT OF FIDDLING THE VAT RETURN. HEAR THE LAIRD CURSE THE RAIN, RECITE BURNS AND BLESS THE INVENTION OF THE CARAVAN. TEAS. TOILETS. ADDERS.

Taking Time Off

A Cabaret at the Races

The horses are magnificent, of course, but above all it is the
people who make a day at the races such a splendid cabaret.

This week I observed a new archetype to add to the great
gallery of characters to be seen at any big race meeting – the
sheik. His horse won a race and he came to collect the cup with
an attractive woman on either side of him, dark glasses shading
his eyes from the February drizzle, moustache concealing most
of the bottom half of his swarthy face.

He looked delighted with his win and he had a couple of
losers later in the day which made him seem human, but the
interesting thing was that he caused no stir among the throng
because racing crowds, more than any others, have learned over
the years to absorb every type and every class without a single
sideways glance.

The Arab collected his cup in the same enclosure as Indians,

Greeks, the Queen Mother, hairdressers, bookies, farmers, crooks, and lawyers have collected theirs in the past.

Owners, I thought as I leaned on the paddock rail, fall into two categories. Those who love horses and those who love being owners. At a National Hunt meeting, the former, mercifully, predominate; but the relationship between owner, trainer and jockey must be pretty sticky at times. It does not show much when they are saddling up and full of confidence. Truth outs when the race is run and lost.

The faces round the ring – and in the enclosures, on the rails, at the bars, around the bookies – are by Damon Runyan out of Rowlandson.

People turn themselves into caricatures of their backgrounds with an unashamed ease that would make a satirist's life very easy. Tweed-suited old boys with veins in their noses like lines on a map of the Balkans; ladies in sensible coats who know more about horses than anyone else around; stewards in bowler hats; a Yorkshireman in amazing blue-checked trousers.

Just after I had observed the sheik, I fell into conversation in the bar with a man called Casey, an enormous Irishman, complete with glass of Guinness, who knew for sure what would win the three o'clock and would generously be prepared to share the secret with me for the price of a drink.

Out in the stand a few moments later, I sat in front of an enormous cockney, with a face out of *The Sweeney* and two similarly solid-looking mates; he had staked £50, he told his friends, on a 10–1 shot which proceeded to lead from start to finish of the three miles and sailed over every one of the sixteen fences as if they were knee-high. The man behind me shouted himself hoarse; then took an age deciding whether to take his mates to the bar for 'a bottle' before or after collecting his money.

Down among the bookies, things happen faster than they do in the Members' Enclosure. Bank notes slide rapidly from palm to palm, men are thinner, women rare, vowels shorter. One big wager on an outsider and fifty hands shoot up simultaneously to drop the odds.

In the stand, white gloves fluttering like pigeons, a tic-tac man called Fingers flashes vital financial messages to the men below in the cashmere coats. As out of place as a canary at a cat show, a languid youth, decked out in blue suit, weighty binoculars, suède boots and the uniform brown trilby – as chinless as only the English can be – places a bet with Honest Alf. His girlfriend – tweed cap, blue Husky – shivers like a whippet while she waits for him.

Neither causes a flicker of interest. If they walked into Honest Alf's local in Dagenham, they'd be laughed out into the street. Another example of racing's delightful eclecticism.

Caps, hats, binoculars, every eye turns to the track as three horses come to the last fence together. The whips smack as they land, one of the jockeys yells something at his rivals, the colours of their caps and sweaters look bright in the fading light. Jump jockeys must be some of the most underestimated athletes in sport. Their bravery, punishing schedules, strength, balance, co-ordination, fitness, reflexes and coolness, should put them in the Superstar bracket and certainly in the supertax category.

Perched high on their horses, mud flying in their faces, it is hard to believe they are in the same business – entertaining the public through sport – as all those millionaire golfers and petulant tennis players.

On the way out an old cavalry officer falls into step beside me. 'Good racing today. Good meeting. Good horses,' he says. 'Makes a break from the farm, eh?' I agree, and add: 'Good people too.'

Maximum Sport, Minimum Blood

Last year I could not shoot straight because it was so perishingly cold all the time.

The year before that, the trouble was some well-intentioned shooting school instructor who had told me to aim off a yard to the right of every bird I fired at and I never got used to deliberately blazing away into space.

The year before that, I suspected I was consistently drinking too much at lunchtime and the year before that I was certainly not drinking enough.

The preceding season was the first in which I tried to shoot with my left eye closed, which naturally took a lot of getting used to; before that I was not shooting frequently enough; before that I was doing too much . . . and I think the year before that was the one when I seemed to buy box after box of blank cartridges.

This year I have run dry of excuses. I had a cast put on the gun, the stock shortened and a couple of lessons at the start of the season; I have had just the right amount of kind invitations which I have accepted with enthusiasm; I invested in fur-lined boots and a nice warm waistcoat; birds have flown straight and true . . . and still I miss them.

I am the perfect answer to the anti-bloodsport brigade: a maximum of sport and a minimum of blood.

Perhaps things have improved fractionally. This year I have never stood at the end of the wood and prayed that nothing would fly over me, an abject state to which I have been reduced in the past. Nor do I look at my neighbour after a bird at which I have shot has fallen, assuming that he fired at the same bird at the same moment as me, thus accounting for the creature's timely end.

My grandfather was one of the great shots of the turn of the century. In common with many of his contemporaries he kept a meticulous record of not only what he shot, but also how many cartridges he used. He was thus able to produce shooting's equivalent of the bowling analysis with an average in the final column of cartridges per bird.

He would turn in his grave if he could see his grandson's figures. Every bird costs me at least ten cartridges. It amazes me sometimes, at the end of a drive, to look at all the empty red cases pointing accusingly up at me from the ground. I can usually bury a few in the plough with my heel before the pickers-up come round, but grass or a hard frost leaves me with no escape.

'Anything to pick?' 'Er, no, I'm all right, thank you,' which leaves open the faint possibility that I shot a dozen which have already been picked. I know that nobody is fooled.

The reason things are marginally better this year is that a friendly shooting instructor finally told me to get a bend put in the stock of my gun and a couple of inches taken off the end of it (inches that were originally put there on the advice of another instructor). A cast on a stock costs almost nothing and takes almost no time. I wish I had had it done ages ago.

Shooting schools, I could write a book about. If ever they want a consumers' guide to shooting schools, I can write it.

From Ohio to Northolt I have been to shooting schools and I still cannot hit clay pigeons, never mind pheasants. Shooting schools are staffed by amazingly patient, understanding men who believe – quite correctly – that their first duty is to give you confidence. It is rather like psychotherapy: if they cured you the first time they saw you, they would all be out of work.

This week, elder son walked round the farm with a gun for

the first time in his life. So far he has missed one rabbit, one pheasant and one pigeon. He loved it.

After twenty-five years of missing, I still enjoy it, when I'm not crying with embarrassment or cringeing with shame. I tell myself that if I hit everything it would all seem too easy and become less fun. I'm sure that next year I shall find out for myself whether that is true. Roll on next season.

A Wayward Lad

Were you there when Jonjo won the Gold Cup? With your own two eyes did you see his red jersey close the gap on Wayward Lad – Wayward Lad who had the race won at the last – close the gap and stride on to win by a length?

Did you see it? Not on the box, not through the words in the newspapers afterwards but there at Cheltenham, part of the whole roaring, wonderful, raw afternoon.

Cheltenham? Isn't that the meeting where you get brayed at by green-wellie-wearers and breathed on by drunken Irishmen? Doesn't it usually snow? Aren't the crowds appalling, the traffic like Dublin in the rush hour, the parking as easy as Knightsbridge during Harrods' sale?

Cheltenham? Wallies and Paddies and £20 to get in? But it could not be worse than home – two more ewes with prolapses, the spares for the tractor not yet delivered and November's invoices still to be entered up in the books. There is nothing to compare with the hard reality of a bookmaker dropping your £5 note into his satchel if you are wanting the mind taken off the chimerical world of prolapses and ploughs.

And here we are in the last couple of furlongs with Wayward Lad leading them home and my fiver apparently safe on his nose. And here is Jonjo, all Ireland's favourite son, bringing Dawn Run back from beaten as deftly as a pick-pocket lifting tenners from hand-bags. And there was a bit of that going on as well.

Jonjo's bloody done it. Jesus, the roof will lift off the stand. Irish tweed hats, generally worn low over the eyebrows, are soaring into the grey air with no thought to where they might land or whether ever they will be seen again, no planned re-entry. 'Jonjo' roar a thousand well-lubricated throats.

'Jesus, Jonjo's bloody done it,' jigs the blue-eyed, black-curled caricature of a Limerick man in front of me, and even those of us who have seen the winnings from £5, very reasonably invested, disappear in those last few strides have to cheer the manner of its disappearance.

Then all those battered sheepskin coats, and tweedy hats and even a few brown trilby numbers, bought from the outfitters in Cirencester High Street, all together they turn their backs on the course and charge for the collecting ring.

A run and a jostle and a hundred broken, tinkling, glasses later they reassemble to welcome steaming Dawn Run, and laughing Jonjo, and the radiant Queen Mother, and lovely Mrs Charmian Hill, and a gorgeous red-head in an ankle length coat of outsize crimson and black checks who must have been supplied by Central Casting out of their 'Irish Beauty' category, and a fast-moving priest wearing a scarlet and white baseball cap – to welcome them all and a thousand more to the collecting ring – welcome them with 'Here we go, here we go, here we go . . .' a roar of joy and happiness warm enough to distil the chill Gloucestershire mist into potheen, the kind of explosion of triumph which only sport and battle bring.

And back at the bars afterwards, there was the stuff itself – amber whisky, gold champagne, black Guinness, all the colours of celebration. And don't they say there is more drink spilt at Cheltenham than ever is drunk at effete, home counties' Ascot?

And they are not just boozers and betters and brawlers, the Irish. They are philosophers too; and what triggers off either the brawling or the philosophy, and you can never predict which, is the holding of a straight glass of Guinness in the fist. And it was a philosopher in, I think, the Arkle Bar, who summed it up: 'The best you can hope to do in life, sir, is to add a little to the sum of human happiness, you know. And to-day, sure Jonjo did his best. For the happiness, you had to be here to see it.'

The Arable Man with a Passion for Cowes

Some farmers take more than strictly agricultural factors into account when planning their years and forming their cropping policies. It may shock the conscientious, but it is true.

I know a man who got out of sheep completely because lambing prevented his skiing when he wanted to; shooting can seriously delay winter cultivations; and a couple of weeks ago I met an arable man who so arranged his system that he is always free at the beginning of August to spend ten consecutive days racing his boat on the Solent.

For several years he grew only winter wheat and never cut any of it until Cowes Week had finished. Now he risks about a hundred acres of winter barley – on early land – which he reckons to combine before the sailing starts in earnest. After his nautical natural break, he returns invigorated to do battle with his wheat.

'Avoid spring barley like the plague,' he advised me. 'Especially in an Admirals' Cup year. There was a time when I thought I might have to move to Scotland and grow only spring barley, thereby putting off the whole harvest operation until Cowes had finished; but I decided eventually to stay down south where the weather is more forgiving and one missed day is less likely to mean disaster.'

He had his tongue stuck firmly between his wisdom teeth, of course, but his attitude has much to commend it. Selling up and moving seems a little extreme, but I have always been told that it makes more sense to be a little late cutting than too early.

Given the twitchy state most of us get into when the weather is changeable and crops are nearly fit, it is probably a sound investment to get off the farm completely for a few days, leaving the combine key under the beer mug in the kitchen where no one will find it.

That way, you might spare yourself those long, painful, sunny days when the sound of your neighbours' combine moving peacefully around the field is drowned by the noise of your dryer struggling to get the stuff below nineteen per cent.

Old Eli has a contemporary proverb which sums up the situation:

> 'When first 'e think thy corn be fit
> Go down the pub for a good long sit.'

And my Cowes week acquaintance worked on the theory that:

> 'The sun will dry the wheat for nowt
> While you're tacking to windward and going about.'

If you are looking for an excuse for taking part in Cowes Week (you guessed it . . . I need one), you can always take a leaf out of the Army's book in a section entitled 'adventure training', sub-paragraph headed 'character, the forming of'.

Another man I met was a soldier who this year will have twelve weeks sailing all paid for by the Army – or rather, the tax-payer.

There is no doubt that spending three hours trying to get round a buoy with the appropriately depressing name of Gurnard, while the wind dies and the tide gathers strength against you, does form your character. Whether it makes you a nicer or a nastier person is more open to question.

The point is that it is just as important that farmers' characters should be formed as soldiers'. Farmers have to lead men, fight enemies, wrestle with frustrations, take decisions fast, accept failures slowly – just like soldiers. The similarities are strong enough to justify character-forming on a massive scale. Things break at crucial moments on boats as well as balers; people make mistakes with spinnakers which can be as expensive as those they make with sprayers; and a crew is a team as surely as a squad of farm employees.

There are more aspects of the Isle of Wight than Cowes and they can be relevant, too. If you think a day's rain in August is bad for your cashflow and turnover, think what it does to the economics of the whelk stall on the end of Shanklin Pier.

There is plenty of agriculture on the island, as well. The arable man who never misses Cowes Week has one golden rule which he says he must obey if he is to get through without destroying his peace of mind.

'Never sail too far up the Medina,' he told me. 'If you do, you will soon come within sight of the Isle of Wight Grain Storage silos; you might even catch sight of the dust rising as the lorries and trailers discharge. It can ruin your sailing day.'

Blazers, Club Ties, Tattoos and Lurchers

'You must come to the Lambourn Lurcher Show; it's a laugh a minute.'

'I wouldn't go near Lambourn on Lurcher Show day; more rogues gather there than in Wormwood Scrubs.'

In the face of such conflicting advice, the best thing seemed to be to put the wallet in an inside pocket and go.

The Show is held on the hills above Lambourn, a beautiful open setting with the Downs rising all around, some of the best gallops in Europe on the skyline and prehistoric tumuli in the foreground. This year the sun shone unhesitatingly, the crowd was thick but not too thick, the noise of barking was unrelenting and the police were notable only by their absence.

A lurcher, I discovered, is a cross between a collie and a

greyhound. One expert insisted that it should also have 'a bit of deer' in it, which apparently means he looks for deerhound blood in the breeding; and sure enough this year's champion was a three-way cross. For the purposes of judging, the dogs are split into large and small, smooth and rough dogs, and bitches, young and old; and some, it must be said, appeared to have some very mixed bloodlines.

I got some very dirty looks when I asked at what point a hybrid becomes a mongrel.

Showing took place in the morning and led to the kind of disagreements about favouritism and prejudice which spoil all showing, whether of dogs, cattle, giant onions or Miss World.

'You wouldn't expect him to give it to a smooth dog, would you? Not when he's always been keen on rough bitches,' said an enormous beer-bellied gypsy to his diminutive stable-lad companion, reminding me of the Lambourn resident whose dog was champion rough bitch one year – and mysteriously disappeared from her kennel a week after the Show.

Good lurchers are much sought after – by fair means and foul – and used for coursing and rabbiting. Hence the notable increase in excitement after lunch, which most of the crowd took in the beer tent, when the racing after a dummy hare began.

In heats of eight the dogs raced uphill over a straight 220-yard course. There were classes for every kind of dog, heats and semi-finals and finals, until well into the evening. Some dogs chased the dummy, others chased each other, others strolled unconcerned away from the start and straight back to their distraught owners.

Whatever they did, they barked; and the spectators' dogs barked back; and those which did not bark, yapped or growled or bared their teeth menacingly at each other.

The dogs were interesting, but not nearly as interesting as the people. There is some link, which I have not fully understood, between lurcher owners and the horse-racing fraternity, and the throng was very much like a small version of the Derby Day crowd.

There were men in Panama hats, blazers and club ties; and men in cut-off jeans, tattoos and little else. There were women in sensible tweed skirts and headscarves; and women in slit black satin numbers. There was at least one big Easy Rider Harley Davidson and one Ferrari in the car park. There were accents from Epsom, Eton and Aberystwyth.

One day a Sunday colour supplement will feature the Lurcher Show and point out the similarities between the Lambourn crowd and the throngs that used to head out of London to watch bare-knuckle fights and cock-fights – the mixture of fops and fighters, Corinthians and crooks must be about the same now as then.

As the racing started to pall, the crowd gravitated towards the surrounding stalls selling purse net rings, fox nets, ferret harnesses, lurcher puppies, exotic poultry, tracer-bleepers for terriers and similar goods definitely not stocked by Harrods.

Centrepiece of one stall was a catapult the like of which I have never seen before. It had a pistol grip and, in the hands of the wrong person, could be used for all sorts of skulduggery.

All of which goes some way to explaining why one group of people was not at all in evidence. I saw only one local farmer during the day, because farmers suffer too much from lurchers chasing sheep and their owners chasing pheasants and everything else that moves. A man from Gloucestershire told me his dog had been put down the day before for killing eleven of his neighbour's ewes.

To set against that, thousands of pounds have been raised by the Show for charities; and even the losers enjoy themselves.

Match of the Day

The cat likes the autumn. I don't. The only thing that makes it tolerable is football and I would like to recommend a visit to a football match to anyone who currently feels as glum as I.

The long, dark evenings provide the cat with plenty of opportunity to gaze into the flames of the fire, a sight she finds even more fascinating than her other great enthusiasm – water emptying from the bath.

After all the rush of harvest, cultivation and drilling, I find the evenings depressing and the turning leaves fill me with a sense of death and decay. Spring seems five long years away, not five short months.

The busiest time of the year, complicated by a trip to the Soviet Union, has had my adrenalin going for weeks on end, but the autumnal gloom is not just a reaction to that; it happens every year when the clocks change. It is connected with the start of the winter routine, feeding and bedding cattle, feeding and bedding yourself, sawing logs, trying to keep warm and dry. Nothing in the farming year beats the dreariness of opening up the silage clamp for the first time, something that those poor long-suffering men in the north and west had to do weeks ago.

There is no silage this year for me, just 1,200 big bales stacked and headed for the oven. What will the cattle look like when they come to the calving after a winter on this strange foodstuff: wheat straw that was battered by rain and baled between showers? Is this another reason for depression?

Even the sight of the neat tilth and shooting wheat does not lift my prevailing mood, because the memory of the messy end that awaited last year's optimistic little plants is too fresh in the mind. Fresh too are my final yield figures – not two tonnes anywhere – and my ADAS man's written report: 'Both wheat and barley yields were low compared to the average . . . there does not seem to be an immediate explanation.'

The shooting winter corn roughly coincides with the start of a different shooting season, and many farmers seek escape from reality in the thud of a falling pheasant and the slosh of the lunchtime claret. Perhaps one reason why I no longer choose shooting as my escape is that it presents a serious risk of encounters with other farmers who want to tell me how well their business is going. I don't want to know. I have never yet met a farmer at The Dell, Southampton FC's picturesquely named home. Once or twice a fortnight through the winter I shed all responsibility and go there; occasionally I indulge in the same thrill of exploration that hooked Columbus and Magellan and voyage to exotic parts such as Highbury, Loftus Road or Swindon.

There is a risk, of course – not of violence, there is more violence dipping the sheep – but of defeat which will cause even deeper depression. Also, a player may play as inexplicably badly as my wheat has yielded. If he is on your team, this leads to sullen silence or mocking laughter.

If he is employed by the other lot, you can tell him what you think of him. You CAN do that to wheat too, of course. You CAN stand out in the middle of a field and shriek 'AQUILA, YOU'RE RUBBISH, YOU ARE,' but it is not half as satisfying as shouting it at a bloke who is earning £60,000 a year yet, judging by the look of him at about 3.10pm on Saturday, trains in a nightclub on vodkas.

When Southampton delivers the goods the subsequent week glows even if the cattle are up to their hocks in mud. The other day they – Southampton, not the cattle – beat Tottenham Hotspur 1–0. Spurs ran on like supermen, their very names enough to fill you with foreboding: Waddle, Roberts, Galvin, Ardiles, Clemence, Falco.

After five minutes, we realized they were human; after forty, they looked over-paid, under-trained and ordinary. There is no possibility of sitting through a live first-division match and thinking of the farm. Where else can you regularly roar aloud with pleasure, shout encouragement, tease the incompetent? Catharsis: outlet to emotion afforded by drama. That's it exactly. Cats don't need it – flames provide no drama.

Shows Are The Business

The Thelwell Season is Here Again

'Can you let me have some wheat straw to bed my pony?'
   'We need some grazing for Wrinkles, and wondered . . .'
'Do you grow oats?'

'That field of yours by the road would be ideal for a gymkhana.'

Yes, it's the Thelwell season again, when ponies fat and fatter, docile and snappy, fast and slow, emerge from their stables and paddocks and sheds into the glory of Pony Club Camp, and a season of shows and gymkhanas that must bring a gleam to the eye of every horse-box manufacturer in the country.

It is a completely new world. Ever since, at the age of six, I took the maximum possible drop from the back of a Shetland – it must have been all of three foot – I have kept well away from ponies and horses of every kind. Occasional investments in absolute cast-iron certainties priced at 33–1 have done nothing to re-establish my faith in the animals.

The situation altered when my elder son became hooked on riding, a powerful drug but one which only rarely proves fatal. A rigorous course of lessons, intended to cure him of his addiction, had quite the the reverse effect and led instead to stage two of the problem – a pony of his own.

That brought us to the ridiculous sight of me, him and the pony all gathered around an open book early last year, staring uncomprehendingly at a page marked 'putting on the bridle'. The only member of the trio who had tackled this problem before was the pony, and luckily he proved a good tutor.

Through the summer the three of us acquired the basics – tack and grooming became a routine, and we were quite happy trotting around the farm in the evenings. Elder son started to do quite a passable imitation of Pat Eddery crossed with Mark Phillips and the pony discovered a nice bit of grazing outside the pub.

Then we were suddenly pitched into stage three of the problem by a suggestion that pony and son should enter a show: and they returned home bearing that prize beyond price – a rosette.

Pony addicts are one thing: rosette addicts are in a much more serious condition, which soon leads to stage four of the hang-up – the Pony Club. This year Pony Club Camp fell neatly into the long spell between hay and harvest which left farming farmers all over the country with precious few excuses for ducking out.

If bridles were a mystery, the world of the Pony Club was an enigma.

Take, for instance, Major Faudel-Phillips' System. This is a method of learning the 'points of a horse and the seats of ailment and unsoundness'.

There are seventy-four of these, and to somebody still rather proud of knowing the difference between a forelock and a fetlock, they come as a bit of a shock. Did you know that the spavin is the same thing as the bog? Could you point unerringly to a pony's ergot? Can you talk confidently about tread, strike, corn, and windgall?

And not only do ponies appear to grow more complicated at this stage, but so does their saddlery. Numnahs, martingales, bridoon and Banbury-action bit-lip straps all make their threatening appearances.

You only have to watch a relaxed young mother discussing gardening with a friend while nonchalantly plaiting a pony's tail and watching her youngest daughter notch up another clear round to know that you will never really master it all. An empty feeling of complete inadequacy creeps over the novice father, a feeling that grows much deeper when he finds himself in the stable before breakfast struggling to combine mane, thread, needle and rubber bands into those smart, tight little plaits that other ponies have.

But it is not all suffering. Reluctantly, I have become convinced that life with a pony teaches children invaluable lessons about responsibility, kindness, firmness and good sense. Gymkhanas, as well as being immensely enjoyable, teach them to take the rough with the rosettes. And there is a lot to be said for anyone who can painfully fall off time after time, yet hold back the tears and climb back on.

So all in all, when the Thelwell season opens again next year, I shall be more ready to seek out those few remaining bales of wheat straw and try to find a bit of grazing.

To be honest, I am quite looking forward to it . . . apart from anything else, many of those young mothers who turn out such attractive ponies are very easy on the eye themselves – and very kind to ham-fisted fathers.

Beer for Breakfast

I had the good fortune to meet Cortina Jones on his stand at the Royal. Had I been brave enough, I could have met his brother Granada, too.

Cortina has the British agency for the new made-in-Albania stubble plucking and briquetting machine. You must have seen it. In one pass it pulls the individual straw stalks from the ground – roots and all – chops, processes and presses them into high-density briquettes which can be burned in solid-fuel stoves, fed to cattle, re-incorporated in the seedbed or sold in boxes as high-fibre breakfast cereal.

It was lunchtime on Thursday when I was ushered into his presence, and he looked in need of some high-fibre something himself, for, as he explained to me, it had been beer for breakfast since the Monday.

He was quite prepared to take me over to meet Granada, but

the prospect filled me with the same feeling of foreboding that I get before a funeral.

Over a can of something cold he told me about the rigours of Royal life, the strain of being polite to competitors, the endless pep talks to staff and agents, the worry of the visit by the Albanian manufacturers on the Tuesday, the sticker-hunting kids, the booze.

'How has business been, though?' I asked.

'Not too bad,' he said, but I knew he meant excellent.

We were interrupted by his beautiful public relations director, personal assistant, astrologer, and masseuse who wanted to know whether he would agree to send a tonne of briquettes to Africa, and while he discussed it with her I was able to look at some of the brochures he had given me.

'Would you like to come over and meet Granada?' she asked when they had finished, but although she smiled winningly I was not man enough to accept.

Cortina told me all about the newest project on which the Albanians are working, a stubble plucker powered by briquettes it has made itself.

'The briquettes are fed into a boiler and the whole thing is steam driven,' said Cortina. 'They have only to get over the environmentalists' objections to the smoke, and outwit the oil companies' dirty tricks departments, and they are in business.'

It seemed to me that it would be the best product line he had almost handled since he failed to import the automatic sheep shearer (ASS) from New Guinea. You remember the automatic sheep shearer – it looked a bit like a chicken plucking machine.

'One plucking thing after another,' said Cortina.

I never knew the truth of why he had to give up the ASS. Some say the animal rights folk were against it. Others claim the Australian Shearers' Union threatened to run him through one himself if ever a single machine left the New Guinea Agricultural Research Centre where it was developed.

They are awful Luddites, the Australian shearers.

It was getting hot in the back of the stand as I came to the end of my time with Cortina, but he kindly gave me a plateful of briquettes to eat and found another can. Revived, I seriously considered accepting his offer of an introduction to Granada, but, wisely I think, I decided against it.

The thing is, I know what line Granada has been in ever since he gave up importing crop chemicals from Nicaragua. He has gone up market and presides over a huge permanent stand near the Main Ring. His business now is milking parlours and I just did not have the moral strength to face Granada Jones and the temple of doom. It must have been the heat.

An Endangered Species

Somerset hedgerows and fields provided shelter and resting places for an uncommon species of wild life towards the end of June. The area around Glastonbury was particularly seriously affected and in some cases the police were called by worried citizens to control the intruders.

Passing motorists reported hundreds of them lining the road-sides holding out rough cardboard notices reading 'Manchester', 'Scotland', 'Scunthorpe', 'M5', and 'anywhere please'.

The fans from the Glastonbury pop music festival were starting the long migration back to their summer quarters, full of feelings of gratitude, I hope, towards the farmers who provide the habitat for their rituals.

Among the many observers from the wildlife funds and natural history societies, wholefood co-operatives and under-water childbirth educational trusts, free Mandela and ban aspirin groups was Norbert Intensely-Serious. Norbert, you will remember, made his name with his postgraduate sociology thesis entitled *Yoghurt – The Symbol*.

He is currently working on a study of the differences between hippies and pop fans. To those like myself, who heard the Rolling Stones live in 1965 and were closet flower-power people for three weeks in the summer of '66, Norbert is a fascinating man to talk to.

'Where the pop fans have been so clever,' he says, 'is that they have got themselves listed as an Appendix II species under the Berne Convention. This means that the government must "ensure the conservation of their habitats" (Article 4(1)) and "prohibit the deliberate damage to or destruction of breeding or resting sites" (Article 6 (b)).

'The Convention also prohibits all forms of deliberate capture, keeping or disturbance of Appendix II species but our Govern-ment has gone further; it has a deliberate policy of encouraging alternative farm enterprises, and the provision of breeding and resting sites for music lovers is definitely smiled upon by the Gummer/Jopling clique.

'The hippies must get themselves designated as an Appendix II species in the way the music fans have done. There is no question that they are endangered, ask any Wiltshire policeman; and all sorts of creatures, from the Squacco heron (*Ardeola ralleoides*) to our very own dear Great Crested Newt (*Triturus cristatus*) have had no problem in getting on to the list.

'Once they are in Appendix II, they have only to prove that Stonehenge is a traditional hippy breeding ground (and that should not be difficult) and they have got it made.'

A Government spokesman today refused to comment on the reasons why pop fans are officially encouraged, while hippies are asked to move along, but he did say that Whitehall was keen to see Norbert's analysis of the difference between the two species. The suspicion remains that the G/J clique cannot tell them apart and it must be admitted that to the casual observer they look much the same – untidy and joyless. To an expert such as Norbert they are as different as Stonehenge and Glastonbury Tor.

Meanwhile the Somerset fields stay open for the music lovers while Stonehenge remains ringed by barbed wire and patrolled by police Land Rovers . . . and Norbert has hitched his way from Glastonbury to Stoneleigh.

'For many years I have been getting reports of a ritual annual gathering in Warwickshire,' he said. 'A species known as farmer (*Agricola agricola*) apparently converges on a traditional site there every summer to drink and shout, parade and trade. It is fortunate that they are in Appendix II, along with the smooth snake and the otter, the corncrake, merlin, and newt, for otherwise they would undoubtedly be harassed by the authorities. There are definite advantages to being endangered.'

Horns of a Dilemma

Out this month is the first issue of the *Jacob Journal*, official organ of the Jacob Sheep Society. I fell upon it with a thrill of anticipation, certain it would mark the end of the search for that elusive breed society whose members co-exist in peace and harmony. Surely, a band of shepherds who have endured years of teasing about hobby sheep and sheep crossed with goats must have developed the unity typical of oppressed minorities?

Not for them the fearsome hatreds of the great cattle clubs, the kind of naked aggression which will certainly surface as usual at Smithfield next week when that new committee member, Archie Yuppie, is overheard insulting Hilary Hardfea-

tures behind her back, Hilary who has been Southern Area Chairperson for twenty-five years.

My illusions were short-lived. Judging by the *Journal*, Jacob breeders are as contentious as those darlings of this column, the members of Yorkshire Cricket Club Committee. I base my assessment on a no-holds-barred article by the chairman, who signs himself, stiffly, R. F. Bailey.

He writes of 'deplorable examples of very bad showring manners' by his members and says 'exhibitors must realize that when entries for shows are made they tacitly agree to abide by the judge's decision'.

He tells exhibitors to respect their fellow members and their animals and concludes: 'In 1986 I hope we can indicate to the sheep industry that our members' behaviour in the sheep lines has improved as impressively as our sheep have improved in the showring.'

Whatever has been going on? Is the Prime Minister aware of these breakdowns in law and order, these cracks in the fabric of rural society? Will Jacob breeders, like football fans, be required to carry identification cards? Will alcohol be banned from the pens? Must the police presence be increased?

The chairman's picture of dispute and disaffection seems all the more improbable, coming as it does just after a thoroughly delightful article by the society's president, Lady Aldington. Lady Aldington's Christian name is Araminta, and her words carry the combination of charm and zest that her beautiful name suggests.

Each year she retains a fleece in case she dies, in which case, her family is instructed, she is to lie in her coffin on this 'specially beautiful fleece'. A small piece of the wool is to be pinned to the lid so that St Peter recognizes her as a shepherd and therefore, knowing that flocks must be tended seven days a week, forgives her poor attendance at Sunday service.

She gives a brief history of the society's formation in 1969 and drops the marvellous line: 'At this time I was breeding Peruvian Cavies for Harrods.'

Could this be the end of the terrible search? Does the Peruvian Cavies Society operate without acrimony and argument? I doubt it.

Had I known my Bible better, I would not have been in the least surprised that the Jacob Society is as argumentative as any other. Jacob's behaviour with his two wives (who were also his first cousins) and their hand-maidens makes *Dallas* look like *Postman Pat*.

He outwits his brother Esau, and his poor old father-in-law/uncle, Laban the Syrian, with a deviousness that would do credit to a Ewing. More to the point, he acquires his speckled and spotted flocks as a result of some highly dubious manoeuvres with poplar rods and hazel stakes, manoeuvres which would have caused uproar had they ever been revealed to the local branch of the breed society.

With a founder like that, what can today's Jacob Society members expect? Dear Lady Aldington, what are you doing in such company? Should you not have stuck to Peruvian Cavies? Surely you have not been seduced by the way Jacob 'increased exceedingly, and had much cattle, and maidservants, and menservants, and camels, and asses'?

I think I have stumbled on the real reason you miss morning service occasionally. You are nervous you will be subjected to *Genesis*, chapters 27 to 31.

Harvest Home

OUR HERO REAPS HIS JUST REWARD . . . BUT NOT
BEFORE ENDURING TORMENTS AND TRIALS INDUCED
BY THE NEW-FANGLED MACHINERY

Will the Trailer be Forced to Follow On?

'Well, Brian, what do you make of this?'
    'It's certainly getting very dark, Trevor, but the
combine's still moving and I don't believe they'll call it off yet.
What do you think, Fred?'
    'No, they'll not stop yet.'
    'And the combine is coming up to the trailer now, swings in
fast behind it, out goes the auger and the trailer takes the grain
right to the middle. Another near perfect delivery.'
    'Yes, he's certainly got more than the ton there, and that
completes his load; he'll be off to the store with that now, and at
the moment I can't see another trailer in the field, can you,
Brian?'
    'No, there's no other trailer there, but the combine's off again,
moving beautifully through the corn, and what a lovely crop

this is. I can't remember ever seeing a better one and certainly not as early as this, can you, Fred?'

'Well I do remember, on the Australian tour in '66, we went through some fields after Sydney which looked really tremendous, but I've never seen English crops looking like this during the Lords match, that I haven't. One thing I would like to say about this concerns *The Times*' crop survey. Why do they always put Yorkshire in the fourth division? When I played for the county . . .'

'Sorry to break in, Fred, but there is something interesting happening out in the field now. The new trailer was just coming through the gate, and I reckon there was time for two or three more loads before tea, when the combine stopped, right over there by the top hedge. Christopher, can you see what is happening? I'll just have some of this excellent fruit cake while Christopher has a look through the glasses.'

'Thank you, Brian, as you say, it has definitely stopped. There's no doubt about that, and the driver's walking back to the tool box. He seems to know what he's going to need. He's opened the box and taken out . . . the hammer. Yes it's the hammer, that's the heavy hammer, the persuader, not the claw hammer or the one with tape holding the head on. It's definitely the big hammer.'

'Fascinating, Christopher. I can't remember when we last saw the big hammer used on a Thursday afternoon in a field of Huntsman wheat. What's he doing with it?'

'He's walking round to the front of the machine. He's approaching the box – not the commentary box, Brian, the box with the drive and bearing for the knife. He's kicked it, Brian, just once, a lovely right-footed kick with plenty of back swing, and I think I heard a simultaneous oath. Now the covers are off and the hammer's going in, right in next to the bearing, one . . . two . . . three beautiful drives. His second shot was slightly across the line of the drive shaft, but the other two were classics.'

'And the statisticians tell me that the heavy hammer was last used on a Thursday in Huntsman at Headingly in 1936 on a horse-drawn binder, but it looks as if this could be the first time it has ever been used on the knife drive.'

'I like his position. Look at the way he spreads his legs and shoulders as he takes the hammer. An example to all schoolboys. But back to Christopher.'

'The covers are back on again now and his work seems to have done the trick because the machine is moving.'

'I am just wondering, though, whether it hasn't come too late because the sky is now very dark and . . . yes . . . it's raining. Well, Fred, what do you think of this?'

'I do remember once in Bangalore, seeing a man combining on the twenty-third day of the monsoon, but I doubt we'll see anything like that here today.'

'No, they are all coming off – running off, in fact, because it's really pouring down, and the ground staff have not even had time to put a sheet on the trailer. The combine driver just tipped his seat and ran.'

'Yes, that is one advantage of combine cabs which is not much promoted. They do keep the driver dry. I must say this is exceptional fruit cake, though. I expect you can hear the rain coming down now. Have you ever seen rain like this in England, Fred?'

'Oh yes, we get harder rain than this in Yorkshire. I'd call this South of England rain. Pretty wet, really.'

'Oh very good, Fred, very funny, not at all bad for the second week of harvest. Very good.'

'So the situation is that it is raining here in the harvest field with about sixty acres still to cut before the Test is won. An old crow is sheltering under the back of the combine and I see the rain making little paths through the dust on the machine's yellow sides. There have always been storms during harvest and I remember once . . .'

Centre Court Pressure

Pressure. John McEnroe and Jimmy Connors blame their loutishness on pressure. But John and Jimmy do not know what pressure is. They should try farming. They should try growing corn. For one thing, they would feel gentle pressure from the bank manager, something from which they are immune in their present line of business.

Think what obscenities and insults they would need to vent the pressures of a contest which started last September and only now, umpteen rounds later, is approaching the final match – the moment when the combine steps forward to serve a succession of aces . . . or double faults.

The semi-finals, still being fought in some areas, were five-setters against the aphids, but helped by some doubtful line calls from the ladybirds it looks as if that struggle is won and now the pressure is building.

The crops in the south of England look spectacular; they have had all the coaching they can get, now they are on their own with only the weather to beat and a month of watching the barometer and thinking of all the things that could go wrong.

Thunderstorms. 'I don't need this aggravation. Why am I surrounded by this kind of s . . . ?'

Drought. 'Okay you jerk. Where's the f . . . referee? I wanna see the referee. I don't have to take this from a creep like you.'

Three weeks rain. 'You blind b . . . Are you too old to see or something? You stink and this whole place stinks.'

British summers give us Ascot Week, Henley Week, Cowes Week and this week – the week when McEnroe takes on the world. But the cereal farmer's tournament lasts almost a year. In the early rounds he meets mud and rain; the competition narrows to pests and diseases until the final confrontation with the weather. Always at some stage there is a thrilling match against mechanical failure which sets Dan Maskell oohing and aahing like a small steam engine.

This year I had a long drawn out tie-break against the wheel. Anthropologists point to the fact that the Mexican Indians never invented the wheel as an indication that they were a primitive people, but it seems to me more likely that they invented it, together with pneumatic tyre and inner tube, but were sophisticated enough immediately to see the problems it would create and scrapped the idea before it got wrapped up in an expensive, self-perpetuating, government-funded R and D programme.

First of all I thought I had been clever and bought a good second-hand pair of narrow crop spraying wheels – only to discover that tyres to fit them are no longer made.

Then, I was late with the ear-emergence spray because silage making dragged on almost into the first week of Wimbledon – a delay caused by a broken pick-up reel and punctured trailer wheels.

Finally, the overwhelming pressure-inducing wheel news came this week. No wheel would mean no motor car, no motor car would mean no motorway, but beside me now is the dreaded letter from the Department of Transport saying that the route selected for the by-pass is, as feared, directly across the farm.

'Okay you bums, I gotta have the referee out here for this one. This one I just don' believe. How can any f . . . say this is the place for A ROAD for Chrissake. THIS IS A FIELD.'

The wheel has not won the tournament yet. Draft orders and a public inquiry loom. But the wheel is a seeded player, the contest looks one-sided and the touts are not getting much demand for tickets for the final.

Combined Mixed Emotions

A dodgy harvest produces a dog's dinner of emotions – frustration, impatience and ill-temper – but this year I have noticed two new and particularly unpleasant flavours in the mixture.

First, envy: 'The grudging contemplation of more fortunate persons', says the dictionary.

Second, *schadenfreude*: the German word for 'malicious enjoyment of others' misfortunes'.

Those of us who have combines which carry battle honours won in many years' campaigns contemplate grudgingly the sleek modern machines of our neighbours. I was driving back from Southampton on Saturday (we could do no more than draw with Sheffield Wednesday – pathetic) when I saw three identical new monsters parked side by side at the top of the vast wheat field which is the Hampshire Downs in that part of the world.

I felt an unpleasant thrust of naked jealousy run through me. One hundred acres a day would be nothing with equipment like that, and I struggle to do twenty.

But, *schadenfreude*, in the drizzle the three gleaming beasts were getting through the same acreage as my old rattler – zero.

They were green, which seemed appropriate, for do not poets call jealousy 'the green-eyed monster'? My combine is yellow. Or was. Now it is yellow stippled with rust red and dragged with a dark dusty grey. I thought it all very fashionable but my wife tells me that dragging and stippling are no longer smart.

We could wallpaper it, I suppose, although that would be difficult on top where the casing has rusted completely through and the dust puffs out as if the machine were coal-fired. We are good at camouflaging it. When opening up a field and doing the headlands, we bedeck it with branches, twigs and leaves, some of which fall in the engine compartment, dry to kindling and eventually ignite, but most of which dangle from the edges like foliage on a Dad's Army helmet.

The camouflage we collect leads on to another source of envy. What a delight it must be to combine huge, rectangular, tram-lined prairies. Almost every one of my fields ends in a fiddly little triangle in some distant corner. Many have trees in the middle and all have at least one hedge or adjacent wood. With circles round the free-standing trees, triangles in awkward corners and rectangles where possible, this farm seen from space must read like an Egyptian hieroglyphic.

At least the corn here and on the Hampshire Downs is mostly still standing, whereas on the East Anglian prairies it is apparently lodged, battered by storms which we have missed in this part of the world.

We must struggle against *schadenfreude* on this score, and truthfully I take no pleasure from the big arable boys' misfortunes, for it can be no fun having your entire annual income dependent on the weather. Mixed farmers can console themselves that the rain at least makes the grass grow and stretches the grazing.

I must admit to one shaft of malicious enjoyment, though. Rumour has it that Mr Leigh Pemberton, he who castigated farmers for being so unbusinesslike in their financial affairs, has hundreds of acres of the dreaded Moulin wheat. If the gossip is accurate, his budgets and cash flows must be undergoing some stringent reassessments.

As the Governor of the Bank of England, he must be used to doing and re-doing sums, but I do not suppose he has ever before had to rewrite a budget because of a pollination failure.

Harvest Home

D o you feel mentally and physically battered, but also mightily relieved, like a boxer who has just gone fifteen rounds but scraped a win on points?

If so, I guess that you have just finished the harvest and are justifiably relaxing in the satisfaction of a difficult job well done. For a moment you are shielding yourself from the full realization of how little your corn is worth, how much it is costing to dry, how appallingly bad the quality is, and how short a time is left for autumn cultivations.

Already all the troubles of the last few weeks are slipping into a soft-focus background and only the good moments remain, sharply defined in the memory.

You – and I – are afflicted by that marvellous 'harvest home' sensation, a feeling as old as agriculture and as welcome in these days of combines and driers as it was in the days of binders and, before that, of sickles. It can make men do strange things.

I remember my father in the farmyard one day, before breakfast, when the binder was just being put away for the year. All our neighbours had several years previously called in the local contractor's combine; but, although the men had little love for the binder, my father stuck by it – partly out of sentiment and partly through a desire to stay in control of his own harvesting arrangements.

But on this particular morning he said, without forethought: 'I don't suppose we'll need the binder next year. Perhaps we'll get in the combine.'

He went in for his breakfast, but the men, in an acute attack of harvest home euphoria, skipped their meal and spent an hour so thoroughly demolishing the binder that it could never be reassembled again.

'You said we would not need it next year,' they replied, grinning, when my father arrived to view the destruction. 'We didn't want you to change your mind.'

It is a shame that although we still enjoy and deserve the satisfaction of harvest home as much as ever, we no longer have harvest suppers in which the whole farm or village can share in the mixed feeling of joy and relief. I feel these thanksgivings must have had an atmosphere all their own . . . not the wild revelry of a New Year Party, or the carefree familial celebration of a wedding or birthday, but a kind of cheerful, mellow happiness, a deep contentment that all was safe, a feeling in tune with September and the undisputed climax of the farming cycle.

Although I do not remember harvest suppers, I do remember the great days when the thrashing mill used to come.

All the sheaves of oats, so laboriously stooked, and turned in the stook, and carted, and stacked, were lifted one by one from the rick in which they lay so safely and tossed to the man at the top of the mill, the man who ruled all that magnificent vibrating machinery, who would cut the string and slide the bundle head-first down the straw-polished wooden chute into the realms of trays and sieves and separators. That was always a day of celebration, rounded off with a few pints and much good-neighbourliness.

I am not so naïve as to suppose that the past was completely golden. I imagine that in 1646, when the price of wheat slipped to forty-four shillings a quarter (yes, that was about sixty-six groats a stone), there were some pretty long faces casting gloom over the harvest suppers of England. But then again, perhaps I am wrong; perhaps 1646 saw a bumper crop, easily harvested,

and never a thought of the green £ or the price of diesel to blemish a cloudless summer.

Whether it was good or bad, it was not long before only the good moments were remembered, just as already I find it easy to recall the couple of afternoons this year when the sun shone on a combine that moved relentlessly and the grain flowed freely – and harder to recapture my fury when the mornings dawned grey, and the auger broke, and the knife jammed.

One beautiful evening in particular I remember, when we finished the field after dark, the combine's lights probing before it and a solid day's work behind us. We started up the big Lister MEU and had a beer in the barn together before going home all crammed in the Land Rover. It was a good feeling.

Although we deal with diesels and wrenches and noise, and the beer comes in cans, and the horses have gone, we were sharing the satisfactions that farmers and farm workers have shared through the centuries.

If you find this hard to believe, if you feel no romance at all in this, the best time in even a bad farming year, then you are disillusioned indeed.

A Few Words of Explanation

A new dialect is spoken in rural Britain and trickles through this book. It consists of initials and acronyms which fall roughly into four categories.

Eurospeak

The Common Agricultural Policy (CAP) is financed by mythical currencies with names such as Monetary Compensatory Amount (MCA), European Currency Unit (ECU) and European Unit of Account (EUA). Amongst the things they pay for is the Farm and Horticultural Development Scheme (FHDS).

Whitehall talk

Europe cannot be blamed for all the jargon. We have bred some British winners too. The Ministry of Agriculture, Fisheries and Food (MAFF) is responsible for the Agricultural Training Board (ATB), Agricultural Development and Advisory Service (ADAS), Experimental Husbandry Farms (EHFs). All over the country there are Sites of Special Scientific Interest (SSSIs), Environmentally Sensitive Areas (ESAs) and Areas of Outstanding Natural Beauty (AONBs); at Stoneleigh in Warwickshire is the National Agricultural Centre (NAC).

Clubs

Farmers love to join things – the National Farmers' Union (NFU), Country Landowners' Association (CLA), Milk Marketing Board (MMB), Meat and Livestock Commission (MLC) and British Field-sports Society (BFS) to name but four.

Pseudo-science

Once livestock ate hay which was classified as good, moderate, bad or lethal. Now everything they eat is analysed to find out what Metabolisable Energy (ME), Digestible Dry Matter (DM) and Digestible Organic Matter (OM) it offers. ME is measured metrically in Mega Joules per Kilogram (MJ per Kg) and Megacalories (Mcals) . . . but few farmers understand any of this, and certainly not the author of this book.